SAINT ATHANASIUS

Defender of Orthodox Christology
On the Incarnation

A CELEBRATION OF FAITH SERIES

STEVEN R. MARTINS
SAINT ATHANASIUS

To my wife, who always walks in faith with me

~ Steven Martins ~

cántaro
publications

www.cantaroinstitute.org
Published by Cántaro Publications, a publishing imprint of the
Cántaro Institute, Jordan Station, ON.

Cover design: Steven R. Martins
Interior design and typeset: Neytan J. Jiménez

Library & Archives Canada
ISBN: 978-1-990771-17-0

ABOUT THE CÁNTARO INSTITUTE
Inheriting, Informing, Inspiring

The Cántaro Institute is a reformed evangelical organization committed to the advancement of the Christian worldview for the reformation and renewal of the church and culture.

We believe that as the Christian church returns to the fount of Scripture as her ultimate authority for all knowing and living, and wisely applies God's truth to every aspect of life, her missiological activity will result in not only the renewal of the human person but also the reformation of culture, an inevitable result when the true scope and nature of the gospel is made known and applied.

Why would anyone read a book written 1700 years ago? The different context of old books can sometimes make them seem irrelevant. But the truth about God is perennial, and the titanic figure of Athanasius fought a battle against a corrupt church establishment and the Emperor Constantine to refute the teaching of the powerful but heretical Bishop Arius. He was convicted to uphold the truth, regardless of the consequences for him. It was *Athanasius contra mundum,* Athanasius against the world.

He did so, as Steven Martins ably demonstrates in his excellent introduction, to uphold the true teaching of Scripture and the ancient church about Jesus' dual nature. He was both fully God and fully man. Whereas Bishop Arius denied his divinity, in much the same way that Dan Brown also has through his popular fictional novel the Da Vinci Code. Athanasius' bold witness and truthful exposition brought a great light into a time of popular darkness. My prayer is that this new edition may yet fan into flame its ancient power and illumine our own dark days.

—**Scott Masson (Ph.D)**

Associate Professor of English Literature

Tyndale University College, Toronto, ON.

Author of *Romanticism, Hermeneutics and the Crisis of the Human Sciences*

What does it mean that Jesus is "begotten of God" or "the firstborn of all creation"? Is He of the same essence as the Father, or is He an inferior created being? These crucial questions surrounding the doctrine of the Trinity are at the heart of the debate between Arius and Athanasius. In this book Steven R. Martins takes us on a journey and unveils the historical background of the debate, showing that the Trinitarian doctrine didn't begin at Nicaea or with Constantine, but with the teachings of Christ himself and the apostles in the New Testament. I was reminded of the importance of the sound biblical Christology that Athanasius passionately defended and was treated to Athanasius' own words in his *On the Incarnation*, his confession of the historical doctrine of the nature of Christ. This book is a must-read for anyone who loves church history and wants to be encouraged to stand for the truth of foundational orthodox doctrines.

—Nathan Díaz

Pastor and Teacher, Cuajimalpa Evangelical Church, Mexico;
Council member of The Gospel Coalition (Español);
Founding Director of Fish Studios and radio program
producer of Clasificación A

Contents

Series Preface

What is faith? And why should we celebrate it?

OF THE TWO QUESTIONS, the first is the most common, the second, on the other hand, is not given much thought, though it should logically follow. In our pluralistic world, the word "faith" has often been used as a token word for all forms of religious belief and expressions. You'll find it on bumper stickers, billboards, in a series of publications, even in film, music, media, you name it. Faith has somewhat become synonymous for "spirituality", which nowadays can mean almost anything. But is this *true* faith? That is, is this the true definition and understanding of faith, faith in the biblical sense of the term? The short answer is No. Not only does its definition fall short, its directional orientation is also off.

What then is faith? In order to understand what faith *is*, and what faith is *not*, we need to first understand the philosophical concepts of worldview and religion. These concepts, if based on biblical presuppositions, can help provide us with a logically consistent framework of thought, or the parameters by which we can answer these questions faithfully. Otherwise, we're faced with various conflicting definitions without any clear indication as to what is true.

Firstly, a *worldview* is what we all have, it is the lens by which we see the world and interpret its facts and evidences. There is not a single living and thinking person in the world who does not have a set of beliefs or presuppositions concerning reality. As a late apologist defined it, a "worldview" is:

> a network of presuppositions (which are not verified by the procedures of natural science) regarding reality (metaphysics), knowing (epistemology), and conduct (ethics) in terms of which every element of human experience is related and interpreted.[1]

Now, it goes without saying that not everyone's worldviews are correct. If one person believes that the earth is flat, and the other that the earth is round, and we mean in the same sense, only one of the two are right. But who? The two tests by which every worldview must be validated are the tests of logical consistency and correspondence. Is the worldview logically consistent? Does it correspond to reality? The Bible, as God's special revelation, provides us with the *true* worldview, a true set of presuppositions regarding reality, knowledge and ethics that are logically consistent and correspondent to reality. All other worldviews are antithetical to the true worldview and fail in the two tests of logical consistency and correspondence. Why? Because we live and breathe

---

1 Gary DeMar, ed., *Pushing the Antithesis: The Apologetic Methodology of Greg L. Bahnsen* (Powder Springs, GA.: American Vision Press, 2010), 42-43.

in God's world, and thus we can also say, because of the impossibility of the contrary.

Secondly, worldviews are not free and independent from *religion*. On the contrary, our worldview and religion are inseparable. The apostle James wrote to the church that "Religion that is pure and undefiled before God, the Father, is this: to visit orphans and widows in their affliction, and to keep oneself unstained from the world" (Jas. 1:27). In other words, *true* religion is to glorify God in all that we do, in every possible aspect of creational interaction and function —this includes administering the grace of the gospel— the result of consecrating the Lord as holy in the core essence of our being (1 Pt. 3:15). But just as there is *true* religion, as defined by God's special revelation, so there is *false* religion, that which is antithetical to the truth, expressed as worship of creation instead of the Creator (Rom. 1:25). To put it simply, our worldview is the *structure* of our presuppositions, what we believe to be true concerning reality, knowledge and ethics; while our religion is the *direction* of that respective structure, our worship; it is the underlying motive rooted in the condition of the human heart.

The reason that faith has been defined and understood in various ways is because it has been interpreted and expressed from a variety of different religious worldviews, all of which place an emphasis on faith's humanistic orientation (except for the Bible). And while it might seem that some elements of their understanding of faith contain a hint of truth, they are, as a whole system, in the wrong. Having then established the parameters by which we can answer our questions, that is, from the biblical religious worldview, what can we say then to What is faith? And Why should we celebrate it?

The term "faith" in the context of biblical Christianity is used in at least two distinct senses. According to *The Oxford Dictionary of the Christian Church*, it is firstly applied objectively to "the body of truth to be found in the Creeds, in the definitions of accredited Councils, in the teachings of doctors and saints, and, above all, in the revelation contained in the Bible."[2] It is, in other words, a term used to refer to the religious worldview of Christianity. Within this 'objective' faith, there is then, secondly, the 'subjective' faith, which Paul refers to in 1 Corinthians 13:13 as one of the three theological virtues alongside hope and love. *The Oxford Dictionary* explains that this faith "is the human response to Divine truth, inculcated in the Gospels as the childlike and trusting acceptance of the Kingdom [of God] and its demands, and known as 'the faith whereby belief is reached' (*fides qua creditor*)."[3] Whereas other religious worldviews would emphasize subjective faith as a natural human act, the Bible is clear in its teaching that faith is a supernatural act, that is to say, that a Christian can only have faith as a result of God's regenerative work in

---

2 F.L. Cross, ed., *The Oxford Dictionary of the Christian Church*, second edition (Toronto, ON.: Oxford University Press, 1974), 499.
3 Ibid.

his heart (Ezek. 36:26-27; Jn. 1:12-13; 3:3-8; Tit. 3:5). To put it simply, subjective faith is a gift from God for the objective faith of God's revealed truth.

Why must faith be an external gift? Because man, in his sin, cannot of his own volition turn to God in repentance and faith. His sinful disposition prevents this (Jn. 8:34; Rom. 6:20; 2 Tim. 2:25-26; Tit. 3:3). This is not to say that man cannot choose for himself between life and death (Deut. 30:15-20), it is rather that man's will is enslaved to his sinful nature and therefore cannot choose life, the life of Jesus Christ, unless he is first freed from this enslavement (2 Chron. 6:36; Job 14:4; Prov. 20:9; Eccl. 7:20; Jer. 13:23; Jn. 6:65). He will always want to choose death, because he is hostile to the truth of God (Gen. 6:5; Jn. 8:44; Rom. 1:18; 8:7-8; Eph. 4:17-19). This deliverance from his fallen condition is ultimately the work of the Spirit of God, who takes the heart of stone and replaces it with a heart of flesh (Ezek. 36:26), and having freed him from his captivity, with his renewed heart, he is then able to choose the only logical option before him, faith in the Lord and Saviour Jesus Christ and all that that entails (Acts 11:18; 13:48; Eph. 2:8-9; Phil. 1:29; 2 Tim. 2:25-26).

This is precisely why there are so many different religious worldviews in our day and age. Sin has not only caused our alienation from God and our spiritual death, it has also affected, or we might say "infected", the totality of our being, including our intellectual, mental faculties – what theologians call the *noetic* effects of sin.

Instead of interpreting God's general revelation of creation as it truly is, by our fallen and hostile nature we supress the truth and devise for ourselves false worldviews with inevitable god-substitutes (Rom. 1:18, 25). It is partly for this reason that God provided the special revelation of His word as the only authoritative interpretation of His created reality, for without it, we would be as blind men left with arms outstretched in the dark. But when God draws unto Himself men and women by his irresistible grace, these false god-substitutes are abandoned *by* faith *for* the true faith. As John Newton (1725-1807) wrote in his hymn *Amazing Grace*, "I once was lost, but now am found, was blind, but now I see."

If, therefore, faith that saves originates from God —for how else can man be saved?— then a celebration of faith is not only a celebration of what we believe, of what God has revealed —which should be celebrated in its own right— but what God has done to redeem sinful wretches such as ourselves. And what more reason do we need to celebrate faith than the fact that Christ has paid the ultimate sacrifice in order to save us from our fallen, sinful condition and the judgment that awaits the living and the dead (2 Tim. 4:1; 1 Pt. 4:5-6)? Not only does He rescue us from the darkness by forgiving us of our sin, having paid its penalty through his death (1 Cor. 6:20; Eph. 1:7; 1 Pt. 1:18-19; 1 Jn. 2:2; Rev. 5:9), He also reconciles us to the Father and begins the work of renewal and restoration, returning us, by the power of the Spirit and his sanctifying work, to our original state of righteousness and our creational purpose.

If our created purpose is, as *The Westminster Confession of Faith* states, to glorify God and delight in Him forever (Rom. 11:36; 1 Cor. 10:31; Ps. 73:24-26; Jn. 17:22, 24), how can this at all be possible without faith? Does not the author of Hebrews write, "without faith it is impossible to please God"? (Heb. 11:6). It is for this reason also that we celebrate faith, for not only has God granted us the gift of saving faith, but faith makes it possible for us to fulfill our highest end, to glorify God and to delight in Him forever. To celebrate faith then is really to celebrate the glory of God, for true faith rooted in God's word only comes from God, the "author and finisher of our faith" (Heb. 12:2).

A Celebration of Faith is a series that reflects on the lives and contributions of those who have been touched by the grace of God, those who have professed, defended and advanced the Christian religious worldview. And while there are millions of stories to be told, the editorial team behind this series have sought to highlight some of the saints who have both inspired scores of generations towards living lives of faith, and others whose faith, although forgotten, have had a significant impact on the culture of their day. The purpose of this series is to inspire and encourage grace-bought believers towards living out their faith in such a way that demonstrates the truth, beauty and liberty of the gospel and its all-encompassing nature for the furtherance of God's kingdom.

Profiled in this volume is the fourth century patristic, or church father, St. Athanasius (AD c. 296-373), bishop of Alexandria. He is recognized by historians as the chief apologist against the monistic heresy of Arianism, and proved himself to be a proficient theologian, influencing the development and preservation of the Nicene Creed. It could be said that the monumental life of Athanasius is mostly marked by bold and faithful confession, having, in the face of mass persecution, suffered exile numerous times for his defense of the divine personhood of Jesus as the Son of God. He would, in fact, earn the title *Athanasius Contra Mundum* for his willingness to take on the world in defending biblical truth. One of his most influential works, *On the Incarnation*, was written as an apologetic for the doctrine of the eternal Son of God taking to himself, without ceasing to be God, full humanity (Jn. 1:14) for the purpose of the Father's glory and our salvation (Jn. 3:16; 12:28). This classic of Christian theology is included in this volume, preceded by an apologetic for Athanasius as defender, not fabricator, of orthodox Christology written by Steven R. Martins, founding director of the Cántaro Institute. Athanasius, the man credited as being the pillar of the church in the patristic period, stands as an exemplary figure of faith, worthy of being profiled in this series.

It is our hope that the Lord may use this book to help cultivate within the church a greater appreciation for our Christian heritage, for we inherit a great treasure in the faith we have been bought into. May you be inspired through this profile to live your faith boldly, undaunted by the challenges and afflictions of living in a fallen world, knowing that the Lord will sustain you as you seek to be the salt and light of the world (Matt. 5:13-16). And may you be equipped for, and informed as to the nature of the church's mission, to preserve and advance biblical truth, not only in its confession but in its application, for the growth of God's kingdom and for His glory alone.

May God be glorified,
The Editorial Team
Cántaro Publications

Athanasius

Defender of Orthodox Christology

0.1 Introduction

IT WASN'T THAT LONG ago that Dan Brown's *The DaVinci Code*, a historical revisionist work of fiction, became a bestseller. The novel, now forming part of a larger series and cinematic universe, presents an art historian, Robert Langdon, as discovering that the Christological doctrine of contemporary Christianity has no historical foundation.[1] The not so subtle claim is that, Constantine, who reigned as Roman Emperor from AD 306-337, collated, after having commissioned its writing, the New Testament in the fourth century. It was an effort to suppress alternative views of Jesus, namely, any view which relegated the messiah to a mere creature.[2] The historian Michael A.G. Haykin describes Brown's accusation as Constantine astutely manipulating the council at Nicaea "for his own ends, [so] that Jesus was 'turned... into a deity' and became for the

---

1   Gene Edward Veith, "The Da Vinci Phenomenon," *World*, 21, no. 20 (May 20, 2006), 20-21.
2   Dan Brown, *The DaVinci Code* (NY., New York: Anchor Books, 2006), 231-232.

first time an object of worship... [having] shaped the face of Christianity as we know it today."[3] *The DaVinci Code*, however, is fiction, and proves its claims to be nothing more than fiction when compared to historical facts. And yet, in spite of this, it has not prevented scholars and polemicists from attempting to pin a similar accusation of the invention of Christological doctrine on the fourth century church.[4] Constantine may have had political self-interests at Nicaea, but he had no real control over the creed of the church. Athanasius, the young man fighting to defend biblical Christology, on the other hand, could be accused of being the fabricator. There was a time when the pervasive view on the Western side of the Empire was Arianism, and Athanasius fought tooth and nail in his teachings *contra mundum*, against the world, to preserve the belief in the God-man Jesus Christ. It could have been him, or his allies at the council of Nicaea, who fabricated the deity of Jesus.

However, over against the idea of St. Athanasius or the Nicene council as the fabricators of a Christological Christianity, that is, the holy faith centred around and

---

3   Michael A.G. Haykin, *The Church Fathers as Spiritual Mentors: The Christian Mentor, Vol. 1* (Kitchener, ON.: Joshua Press, 2017) 6.

4   American scholar Douglas McCready writes that if such a claim were to, in any shape or form, not necessarily prove identical to Brown's claims in *The DaVinci Code*, "every distinctive Christian belief would have to be discarded" due to it being relegated to triviality and irrelevance in *He Came Down from Heaven: The Pre-existence of Christ and the Christian Faith* (Downers Grove, IL.: InterVarsity Press/Leicester, UK.: Apollos, 2005), 317.

built upon the God-man Jesus Christ, the patristic of the 4th century AD and his later allies at the council defended *orthodox* Christology which pre-dated the fourth century. They ably refuted the albeit popular but heretical and humanistic theology of Arianism, that being the denial of Jesus' deity and eternal nature. I hope to demonstrate in my writing that the evidence for orthodox Christology pre-dates the Nicene council of the fourth century, that denying Jesus the Son as being of same substance as God the Father inevitably leads to monistic theology, and that the sinister intent lying behind these accusations are in fact out of interest of preserving man's radical autonomy.

0.2 Fourth Century Background: The Athanasian and Arian Debate

However, in order accomplish my objective, the historical background of the fourth century church must first be considered. It would do us no good to demonstrate early evidence of doctrinal Christology, the implications of denying the Son's deity, and unveiling the intent underlying the claims of doctrinal fabrication without first understanding the Athanasian and Arian debate which brought these matters to the forefront of the church.

It was the year 318 when Arius, an aesthetic scholar, popular preacher, and student of Bishop Alexander of

Alexandria, protested orthodox Christology.[5] Taking issue with Alexander's sermon, titled "The Great Mystery of the Trinity in Unity," which stressed the unity of Father, Son and Holy Spirit,[6] he launched an attack by teaching that such a unity was a heresy in line with Sabellianism[7] or Modalism,[8] or on the verge of Greek polytheism.[9] Similar to the previous theologians of Alexandria, such as Clement and Origen, Arius was devoted to "speculative theology" and discipled a small group of students tasked with propagating his alternative view on Christ.[10] Very few of Arius' writings exist to this day, but his theology can be reconstructed by his opponents and allies. In one of the surviving letters written to his friend, Eusebius of Nicomedia, he complains that his persecution is because he teaches the *Logos*, the Word,

---

5 Earle E. Cairns, Christianity through the Centuries: *A History of the Christian Church* (Grand Rapids, MI.: Zondervan Publishing House, 1981), 133.

6 Peter J. Leithart, *Athanasius: Foundations of Theological Exegesis and Christian Spirituality* (Grand Rapids, MI.: Baker Academic, 2011), 1.

7 Sabellianism is defined as the belief that the Father, Son and Holy Spirit are three different modes or aspects of God, each manifesting at different points in history, a form of *chronological* modalism, contrary to the orthodox Trinitarian doctrine of three distinct persons within the Godhead.

8 Modalism is defined as the belief that God is not three distinct persons but instead a single person who reveals himself in different modes, Sabellianism would be a category of Modalism.

9 Cairns, *Christianity through the Centuries*, 133.

10 Leithart, *Athanasius*, 2.

existing "by will and counsel" and that "before he was begotten, or created, or determined, or established, he did not exist."[11] According to how some scholars have interpreted Arius, the *Logos* isn't a creature, but neither is he the Creator, for the Creator is the only unbegotten, and for the Son to be begotten means there must have been a time when He did not exist.[12] As Arius himself wrote:

> And God, being the cause of all that happens, is absolutely alone without beginning; but the Son, begotten apart from time by the Father, and created and founded before the ages, was not in existence before his generation, but was begotten apart from time before all things, and he alone came into existence from the Father. For he is neither eternal nor co-eternal nor co-unbegotten with the Father, nor does he have his being together with the Father… but God is before all things as monad and beginning of all.[13]

This does raise the question: If Jesus was not a creature, and he is not one with the Creator God in substance and essence, then what is he? In an attempt to avoid committing the error of Sabellianism or Modalism, Arius blurs the Creator-creation distinction

---

11 Cited in R.P.C. Hanson, *The Search for the Christian Doctrine of God: The Arian Controversy* (Grand Rapids MI.: Baker Academic, 2005), 6-7.

12 Leithart, *Athanasius*, 2.

13 Cited in Ibid., 3.

and inevitably reduces the faith to a form of religious monism. I will address this matter of the negative implications under a later heading.

As opposed to other heresies which emerged from between the first to fourth centuries AD, endured for a time in the life of the church, and then passed into obscurity once refutated, Arianism not only stuck around for much longer but also grew immensely popular with Christians. This was evident in that Arius' doctrine was embodied in prayers and hymns, and the people commonly sung his poems, such as the *Thalia* (meaning Banquet), which went like this:

> …And so God Himself, as he really is, is inexpressible to all.
>
> He alone has no equal, no one similar, and no one of the same glory.
>
> We call him unbegotten, in contrast to him who by nature is begotten.
>
> We praise him as without beginning in contrast to him who has a beginning.
>
> We worship him as timeless, in contrast to him who in time has come to exist.
>
> He who is without beginning made the Son a beginning of created things.
>
> He produced him as a son for himself by begetting him.
>
> He [the son] has none of the distinct characteristics of God's own being

For he is not equal to, nor is he of the same being
as him…[14]

Given that this heresy did not appear to be fading
but instead picked up steam, Bishop Alexander sounded
the alarm by summoning a synod of a hundred Egyptian
bishops. This synod condemned Arius and his teaching as heretical and banished him from Alexandria.[15]
However, far from being the end, Arius traveled from
Alexandria to Nicomedia to stay with his ally and
friend Eusebius, who happened to be the friend of the
Eastern Emperor's wife, and sister to Constantine. Out
of allegiance to Arius, Eusebius summoned a council in
Bithynia, which reversed the Egyptian synod's decision
and declared Arius as "orthodox." This meant that Arius
could return to Alexandria, and he did, with much controversy and quarreling.[16]

To make matters short, as opposed to Brown's
unfounded accusation that Constantine tried to "deify"
Jesus of Nazareth for political means, we instead find
an emperor who was more pragmatic in his faith than
he was convictional. Though he leaned his ear to both
sides, in the end his concern was not doctrine but rather
unity in the Roman Empire. Thus, Constantine resorted

---

14 "Arius – Thalia in Greek and English." *Fourth Century Christianity*. Trans. by William Bright. Accessed June 07, 2018. http://www.fourthcentury.com/index.php/arius-thalia-greek
15 Leithart, *Athanasius*, 5.
16 Timothy D. Barnes, *Constantine and Eusebius* (Cambridge, MA.: Harvard University Press, 1981), 203-204.

to negotiations, first by sending his advisor Ossius to Alexandria, but when matters appeared more heated and complex than the emperor could have imagined, he summoned the bishops from East and West.[17] This is a remarkable event in church history, for it was the first time that the leaders of the church, from throughout the empire, could assemble in such a large scale, it was the first ecumenical council. It was here, at Nicaea in the summer of AD 325, that Arius was condemned by the two-to-three hundred bishops.[18]

Where was Athanasius in all of this? At the time of the council, he served as a deacon in the Alexandrian church and accompanied Alexander as his theological expert and secretary.[19] According to church tradition, Athanasius was first found by Alexander baptizing his friends at the beach when he was a young boy. He thought that Athanasius was playing an inappropriate game, but upon speaking with him, discovered him to be a teachable disciple who earnestly desired to serve the Lord.[20] Athanasius was bright, but was a lot brighter after having received a classical education at the catechetical school of Alexandria.[21] What Leithart notes is that, contrary to Arius:

---

17 Leithart, *Athanasius*, 6.

18 Cairns, *Christianity through the Centuries*, 133.

19 Ibid., 8.

20 T.D. Barnes, *Athanasius and Constantius: Theology and Politics in the Constantinian Empire* (Cambridge, MA.: Harvard University Press, 1993), 10.

21 Ibid.

Though he was able to use the philosophy he knew in anti-pagan apologetics and anti-Arian polemics, Athanasius remained throughout his life mainly a Bible teacher, his most basic convictions, passions, instincts, beliefs, and views shaped not by Plotinus or Stoicism but by Scripture.[22]

The conflict between Athanasius and Arius had not yet come to a head, in fact, Athanasius did not dominate the first council proceedings contrary to popular thought, he was instead subject to his bishop Alexander. He did, however, become recognized as the chief exponent of the orthodox view, namely, the eternity of Jesus Christ and the identity of His substance with that of the Father.[23] The issue he raised at the council was that the debate at hand was a soteriological one, for how could Christ save man from his sin and restore his being if he were only a creature? He must be coequal, coeternal, and consubstantial with the Father.[24] In the end, he was supported by the council, which rejected Arius' views and even that of Eusebius of Caesarea who attempted to find a middle ground between the two positions.[25]

The creed hammered out at the council was as follows:

---

22 Leithart, *Athanasius*, 6.
23 Cairn, *Christianity through the Centuries*, 134.
24 Ibid.
25 Ibid.

We believe in one God, the Father almighty, maker of all things visible and invisible; And in one Lord, Jesus Christ, the Son of God, begotten from the Father, only-begotten,

that is, from the substance of the Father,

God from God,

light from light,

true God from true God,

begotten not made,

of one substance with the Father,

through Whom all things came into being,

things in heaven and things on earth,

Who because of us men and because of our salvation came down,

and became incarnate

and became man,

and suffered,

and rose again on the third day,

and ascended to the heavens,

and will come to judge the living and dead,

And in the Holy Spirit.

But as for those who say, There was when He was not,

and, Before being born He was not,

and that He came into existence out of nothing,

or who assert that the Son of God is of a different hypostasis or substance,

or created,

or is subject to alteration or change

—these the Catholic and apostolic Church anathematizes.[26]

The council, however, in spite of the development and majority agreement of its first Nicene creed, did not dispel Arianism in its totality. In AD 328, when Alexander went to be with the Lord, Athanasius was elected as the next Bishop of Alexandria and brought deeper into the conflict.[27] Constantine thought at this time that this would be the opportunity for Arius to be reconciled with the Alexandrian church, but Athanasius would have no part of it, not when it meant denying the true nature of God and sacrificing biblical truth at the altar of pragmatism.[28] This turned out to be the beginning of many troubles, because with false accusations being made against him from Arian supporters, and pressure from the imperial throne, he was exiled numerous times from Alexandria, each time being reinstated, and each time after that being suspended from his office of bishop.[29] It should be noted that, though Constantine

---

26 "Creed of Nicaea 325, Greek, Latin and English." *Early Church Texts*. Accessed June 06, 2018. http://www.earlychurchtexts.com/public/creed_of_nicaea_325.htm

27 Leithart, *Athanasius*, 6.

28 See Barnes, *Athanasius and Constantius*, 10-14.

29 Hanson, *The Search for the Christian Doctrine of God*, 263.

didn't really take any one side, wavering back and forth between orthodox and heretical doctrine, his successor, Constantius, was an avid supporter of Arius and was more forthcoming. In the early 350s, he summoned two church councils in the Western empire in order to stamp out the Nicene Creed; of course, he didn't succeed.[30] Leading up to this, however, and during the several periods of exile, Athanasius had written several letters, many of which contained anti-Arian polemics. His greatest polemic was *Discourses against the Arians*, which was complemented by his earlier apologetic *On the Incarnation*.[31] The anti-Arian polemics, though rooted in Scripture, angered Constantius to such an extent that he sent Roman soldiers to apprehend the Bishop of Alexandria, but Athanasius slipped away into the wilderness after having ensured his followers' safety, as he did many times before.[32]

What was the central conflict between Arius and Athanasius, the latter carrying on the defense from his predecessor Alexander? Arius taught that the Son knows not the Father because he is not of same substance, he is a creature, and yet not a creature. He may be of similar substance as the Father, as his followers later posited, but he is not one with the Father. He does not even

---

30 Leithart, *Athanasius*, 12.

31 Ibid., 11.

32 See Athanasius, "Apologia de Fuga, 24." *New Advent*. Trans. by M. Atkinson and Archibald Robertson. Accessed June 05, 2018. http://www.newadvent.org/fathers/2814.htm

know his own essence, and as a result, the Father is just as incomprehensible as himself.[33] This is certainly confusing, but it appeared easier to accept than the Trinitarian formulation of God. The principle focus of Arian doctrine, in essence, was the substance of the Son in contrast with that of the Father. Some Arian sects, such as the Anomians of AD 350, stressed the term *anomoios*, meaning completely "unlike," because they found the term *homoios*, that being Jesus as similar, or like the Father, to be too confusing.[34] Basil of Ancyra proposed *homoiousios* as a compromise between the Anomians and the rest of the Arians, that being, the similarity of essence. This would become the definitive doctrinal expression of Arianism.[35]

According to the Arian creed which was later submitted to the emperor sometime between AD 327 and 335, the Son is "produced" by the Father, and all things are said to be made through him.[36] He is, in other words, the created Creator. Athanasius, on the other hand, taught that the Son was eternally begotten, that is, he is the begotten of the Father, but eternally pre-existed. He is not unlike the Father, nor like the Father, but of the same substance as the Father. Though the term *homoousios* is

---

33 Arius' words, as recorded by Athanasius, is cited in Leithart, *Athanasius*, 4.

34 Ibid., 17.

35 Ibid.

36 Rowan Williams, *Arius: Heresy & Tradition*, revised ed. (Grand Rapids, MI.: Wm. B. Eerdmans, 2002), 96.

attributed to the patristics involved in the outcome of the Nicene council, Athanasius reflects the *homoousios* of Jesus and the Father throughout his writings. The majority of the fourth century patristics certainly contributed to the development of the Nicene creed, but it was Athanasius that preserved it afterwards. It can be said that, if Athanasius had not fought Arianism on the grounds of biblical authority, the majority of the empire would have turned Arian, and the Nicene creed overturned. This clearly was not the will of God, such a set back was contrary to his purposes for the fourth century church, instead, in his divine providence the Lord used Athanasius to fight against the world, *contra mundum*, in his defense of the truth of Scripture and its clear teaching. As Leithart writes, "Through most of the history of the church, Athanasius has been regarded as both a theologian of superior ability and a theological warrior of the first order. He is a Christian hero, standing with his Lord *contra mundum*."[37]

Was Athanasius a fabricator of doctrinal Christology? Was Jesus of Nazareth deified in the fourth century when he was originally a human prophet? If someone were to earnestly believe this, they would have to turn a blind eye towards the plain meaning of several New Testament texts and the testimony of the early church. If our ultimate authority for all knowledge is Scripture, then that is where we must begin, and from there, survey the biblical

---

37 Ibid., 15.

interpretation of the church fathers who followed the Lord's apostles in the teaching of the church.

0.3 Pre-Nicene Evidence: The New Testament

According to the scholar Douglas McCready, beginning with the Pauline epistles which are the earliest documents of the New Testament, we find a very high Christology in their theological structure and direction.[38] They not only reveal that Jesus is the Son of God, but that he pre-existed eternally. Colossians 1:15-16, for example, states that Christ is "the image of the invisible God, the firstborn of all creation. For by him all things were created, in heaven and on earth, visible and invisible, whether thrones or dominions or rulers or authorities – all things were created through him and for him." The designation of "firstborn of all creation" has led some to interpret this, such as Arius and the sects that followed him, as meaning that Jesus is himself a creature, created by God prior to the creation of the cosmos.[39] But that is not what Paul is referring to in his writing, instead, he is presenting Jesus as the chief-heir of all creation. New Testament scholar R.R. Melick affirms this by stating that:

> the Jewish concept of the birthright... influences the meaning of the word... The term "firstborn"

---

38 McCready, *He Came Down from Heaven*, 16.

39 R.R. Melick *The New American Commentary: Philippians, Colossians, Philemon,* Vol. 32 (Nashville, TN.: Broadman & Holman Publishers, 1991), 216.

referred to a rite (ritual) that accorded the first son a special place in the family... Paul stated that Jesus 'is His Father's representative and heir and has the management of the divine household (all creation) committed to Him.'[40]

It was Arius' belief that Jesus was the created Creator, but if the divine work of creation *ex nihilo* is exclusively attributed to God, it would be an impossibility for a creation to perform such a creative task. Any Arian leanings would be washed away if Paul's later words in Colossians were heeded. Such as Colossians 1:19, "For God was pleased to have all his fullness dwell in him," which is re-asserted in Colossians 2:9, "For in Christ all the fullness of the Deity lives in bodily form." These texts clearly present Jesus as God without confusing the Father-Son distinction.[41] To blur the Creator-creation distinction, as Arius had done by positing Jesus as the created Creator, would reduce Christian theology to monism, resulting in a distinctionless reality.[42]

There are other instances in Pauline literature where Christ's deity is made mention, such as 1 Corinthians 8:5-6, which states:

For although there may be so-called gods in heaven or on earth —as indeed there are many "gods" and

---

40 Ibid., 215.

41 McCready, *He Came Down from Heaven*, 82.

42 Cornelius Van Til, *Christian Apologetics*, Second edition. Ed., William Edgar (Phillipsburg, NJ.: P&R Publishing, 2003), 32.

many "lords"— yet for us there is one God, the Father, from whom are all things and for whom we exist, and one Lord, Jesus Christ, through whom are all things and through whom we exist.

In contrasting the holy faith with pagan, false religions, Paul preserves the Jewish monotheistic emphasis in likeness to the *Shema*, and directly associates Jesus with the one true God of the Old Testament. This creedal expression stresses not only monotheism but also the unity of creation and salvation, both acts not being possible for a creature, but entirely appropriate for and attributable to the Creator God of Judaeo-Christian theism.[43]

Consider, also, Romans 9:5, which states emphatically and with absolute clarity that "To [Israel] belong the patriarchs, and from their race, according to the flesh, is the Christ, who is God over all, blessed forever. Amen." The clear reading of this text, "the Christ, who is God over all" affirms the deity of Jesus of Nazareth. He is not a mere man, solely a prophet, or a wise sage, he is the Son of God, and God the Son.[44] In fact, the third-century patristic, Origen (c. 185-254), interpreted this as meaning, in the literal sense, that "Christ is the God who is over all."[45]

43   A.C. Thiselton, *The New International Greek Testament Commentary: The First Epistle to the Corinthians* (Grand Rapids, MI.: W.B. Eerdmans, 2000), 636.

44   R.H. Mounce, *The New American Commentary, Vol. 27: Romans* (Nashville, TN.: Broadman & Holman Publishers, 1995), 197.

45   Cited in McCready, *He Came Down from Heaven*, 92.

Paul's epistles aren't the only source of first-century Christology, however, equally important are the gospels which also bear witness of Jesus' deity. Consider, for example, Matthew 11:27 where Jesus says, "All things have been handed over to me by my Father, and no one knows the Son except the Father, and no one knows the Father except the Son and anyone to whom the Son chooses to reveal him." In other words, the Father and the Son have knowledge of each other, and this knowledge is made known to man by the will of the Son. If Jesus were a created being as Arius surmised, who is he to decide who receives the revelation of God and who does not? However, if Jesus were the Son of God, of the same nature and essence as the Father, then he has every right to reveal the truth unto some and not to others. This revelation does not come about by mere chance, or by man's rationalism, but by the will of the Son to reveal himself to the world. Jesus' critical place in the revelation of the Father presupposes his divine authority as God.[46]

John's gospel also exhibits a high Christology, where from the very start it is written "In the beginning was the Word, and the Word was with God, and the Word was God" (Jn. 1:1). This word is explained to be Jesus, for John writes, "And the Word became flesh and dwelt among us, and we have seen his glory, glory as of the only Son from the Father, full of grace and truth" (Jn.

---

46 Leon Morris, *The Pillar New Testament Commentary: The Gospel according to Matthew* (Grand Rapids, MI.: W.B. Eerdmans, 1992), 294-295.

1:14). Haykin explains that these statements, including John 10:30, are to be read "as being more than simply an assertion of his union with the Father in thought and intent. In light of the gospel context it seems to affirm a union of being between the Father and the Son."[47]

These instances of a high Christology in Matthew and John's gospel are but samples, however. The whole New Testament presents the "H.A.N.D.S" of Jesus, that is to say, as per New Testament scholars Robert Bowman Jr. and Ed Komoszewski, that Jesus shares the *Honours* of God (i.e., Matt. 2:2, 11; 8:2; 9:18; 14:33; 15:25; 20:20; 28:9, 17), the *Attributes* of God (i.e., Matt. 2:8-9; Jn. 1:1; 14:9-10; 16:28), the *Names* of God (i.e., Matt. 1:23; 3:3; Mark 1:3; Lk. 3:4-6; Jn. 8:58; Rom. 9:5; 2 Peter 1:11; 2:20; 3:18), the *Deeds* that God does (i.e., Mark 2:7-9; Jn. 1:1; 14:6; Acts 9:2; 19:9, 23; 22:4; 24:14, 22) and the *Seat* of God's throne (i.e., Mark 14:61-64; Lk. 1:33; 1 Cor. 15:25-27; Heb. 12:2).[48] All these traits point towards his deity and go beyond what was expected of any mere prophet in expression, action and thought. Bowman and Komoszewski, in their book *Putting Jesus in his Place*, used the following table (Figure 1.1) to demonstrate the "Paradoxical Person" of Jesus.[49]

---

47 Haykin, *The Church Fathers*, 9.

48 See R.M. Bowman Jr. and J.E. Komoszewski, *Putting Jesus in His Place: The Case for the Deity of Christ* (Grand Rapids, MI.: Kregel Publications, 2007), 23.

49 Ibid., 122-123.

God...	But Christ...	And Yet He...
Is eternal (Ps. 90:2; Isa. 43:10)	Was born (Matt. 1:18)	Always existed (John 8:58; Col. 1:17)
Is immutable (Ps. 102:26-27)	Grew (Luke 2:40, 52)	Is also immutable (Heb. 1:10-12)
Is omnipresent (Ps. 139:7-10)	Was one place at a time (John 11:21, 32)	Could act from afar (John 4:46-54)
Knows all things (Isa. 41:22-23)	Did not know the day or hour (Mark 13:32)	Knew all things (John 16:30; 21:17)
Is incorporeal (John 4:24)	Has a body (John 2:21; Col. 2:9)	Cannot be seen (1 Tim. 6:16)
Is not a man (Num. 23:19)	Is a man (1 Tim. 2:5)	Is also God (John 20:28)
Cannot be tempted (James 1:13)	Was tempted (Heb. 4:15)	Could not sin (John 5:19)
Does not get tired (Isa. 40:28)	Got tired (John 4:6)	Did all God's will (John 17:4)
Cannot die (1 Tim. 1:17)	Died (Phil. 2:8)	Could not have his life taken (John 10:18)

Figure 1.1

The Presbyterian theologian B.B. Warfield is right to say that the structure and direction of the New Testament is "saturated" with the presupposition of the deity of Christ.[50] Jesus came in the form of man, walked like a man, talked like a man, ate like a man, and yet he stood out from amongst men as one far above, as one before, and as one who is not subject to sin and death. It is for this reason that, upon seeing and touching the resurrected Lord, Thomas fell down and said, "My Lord and my God!" (Jn. 20:28). Murray J. Harris, author of *Jesus as God*, states that this expression of worship towards Christ, solely reserved for God, is a view that "prevails among grammarians, lexicographers, commentators and English versions."[51] And for those who think that these passages are nothing more than the elevated views by the few disciples of the "created" person Jesus ought to consider two important evidences: Firstly, Philippians 2:5-11, and secondly, extra-biblical testimony.

Contrary to common thought, Paul did not compose Philippians 2:5-11 but rather quoted a hymn that was sung by the first century church, referred to by scholars as the *Carmen Christi*. In spite of the uncertainty posed by liberal scholars as to the literary nature of the citation, German scholar Ernst Lohmeyer provided a

---

50   Benjamin B. Warfield, "The Deity of Christ" in *The Fundamentals: A Testimony to the Truth,* Vol. 1 (Chicago: Testimony Publishing Co., 1909), 23-26.

51   M.J. Harris, *Jesus as God: The New Testament Use of Theos in Reference to Jesus* (Eugene, OR.: Wipf & Stock Publishers, 2008), 110.

convincing analysis of the passage's "hymnic structure" in his essay *Kyrios Jesus. Eine Untersuchung zu Philipper 2,5-11.*[52] It is a hymn which exhibits a high Christology sung by a community of believers in the early life of the church, serving as a testimony for the consensus of Christ-followers. The text states:

Have this mind among yourselves, which is yours in Christ Jesus,

Who, though he was in the form of God,

did not count equality with God a thing to be grasped,

but emptied himself,

by taking the form of a servant,

being born in the likeness of men.

And being found in human form,

he humbled himself

by becoming obedient to the point of death—

even death on a cross.

Therefore God has highly exalted him

and bestowed on him the name that is above every name,

so that at the name of Jesus every knee should bow,

in heaven and on earth and under the earth,

and every tongue confess that Jesus Christ is Lord,

---

52 See C. Brown, "Ernst Lohmeyer's Kyrios Jesus" in *Where Christology Began: Essays on Philippians 2*, ed., R.P. Martin and B.J. Dodd (Louiseville: Westminster John Knox, 1998).

to the glory of God the Father.

The focus of the *Carmen Christi* is on the example of Christ's humility and self-sacrifice, but it makes two significant "ontological statements about Jesus" as per Haykin, that first he "was in very nature God" (2:6), and secondly, that prior to his incarnation, he possessed "equality with God" (2:6).[53] Faithful to the Old Testament Hebrew Scriptures, the early Christian hymn preserves the insistence of Jewish monotheism and all glory as ascribed to God alone.[54] In its structure and direction, the text cannot be reduced to anything else, the right and true interpretation of the *Carmen Christi*, in the context of Paul's epistle, is the declaration of Christ's nature as being of God himself.

In regard to extra-biblical testimony, that being from pagan sources, we can consider two examples: Pliny the Younger (c. AD 61-113), to begin with, was appointed as Roman governor for the province of Pontus and Bithynia in AD 110. Prior to his governorship, however, he was assigned by the emperor Trajan to remedy the economic misery of the province. Pliny surveyed the ins and outs of provincial life, seeking to develop an understanding of the "ground level before instituting significant changes in the infrastructure of the province."[55] While fulfilling his responsibility to the emperor, he was presented with many Christians, whom, from the empire's perspective,

---

53 Haykin, *The Church Fathers*, 8-9.

54 Bowman Jr. and Komoszewski, *Putting Jesus in His Place*, 58.

55 Haykin, *The Church Fathers*, 11.

were members of an illegal religion which defied the state religion of Rome, that being, the imperial cult. Pliny noted that these Christians refused to submit to Roman authorities when it involved denying their faith, and that the Roman gods were *anathema*, along with worship of the emperor.[56] Reflective of his unethical approach to investigations, which Romans at the time were infamous for, Pliny tortured Christians, and extracted from two ministrae, that is "deaconesses,"[57] that Christians sung "an antiphonal hymn to Christ as to a god."[58] From Pliny's perspective, Christians worshipped Jesus of Nazareth as the God of the Jewish tradition, hence why the Christian church was regarded at first as a Jewish sect.

There is also the satirist Lucian of Samosata (c. AD 125-180) who wrote, in his satirical book *The Passing of Peregrinus*, that Christ "persuaded [Christians] that they are all brothers of one another when they deny the Greek gods (thereby breaking our law) and begin to worship him, the crucified sophist himself, and to live their lives according to his rules."[59] There are several other references than just these two pre-dating the fourth century AD, all affirming that Christians held to an

---

56   Pliny the Younger, "Letters 10.96.8." *Attalus*. Accessed June 1, 2018. http://www.attalus.org/old/pliny10b.html#96

57   Haykin, *The Church Fathers*, 11.

58   Pliny, "Letters 10.96.8."

59   Lucian of Samosata, "The Passing of Peregrinus." *Tertullian.org*. Accessed June 1, 2018. http://www.tertullian.org/rpearse/lucian/peregrinus.htm

orthodox Christology prior to Arius and his perverted doctrine. As Haykin concludes, "Brown's claim that, prior to the Council of Nicaea, Christ was regarded only as a human being" can be countered with the facts of history between Christ's first advent and the Nicene council.[60]

0.4 Pre-Nicene Evidence: The Apostolic Age

The apostles' creed is another example as to the pre-Nicene roots of orthodox Christology. It was believed that each apostle had written a line of the creed, but this is nothing more than a popular legend of church tradition.[61] The apostles' authorship cannot be verified with any certainty. What can be said is that the ancient catechism does rightly reflect the beliefs of Jesus' apostles, as it states:

> I believe in God, the Father almighty, creator of heaven and earth.

> I believe in Jesus Christ, his only Son, our Lord, who was conceived by the Holy Spirit and born of the virgin Mary.
> He suffered under Pontius Pilate,
> was crucified, died, and was buried;
> he descended to hell.

---

60 Haykin, *The Church Fathers*, 10.
61 Ben Myers, *The Apostles' Creed: A Guide to the Ancient Catechism* (Bellingham, WA.: Lexham Press, 2018), 3.

The third day he rose again from the dead.

He ascended to heaven and is seated at the right hand of God the Father almighty.

From there he will come to judge the living and the dead.

I believe in the Holy Spirit,

the holy catholic church,

the communion of saints,

the forgiveness of sins,

the resurrection of the body,

and the life everlasting. Amen.[62]

When comparing this early confession to that of the Nicene council, whether its first draft or its finalized form following the council of Chalcedon, it is evident that what the council had done in order to protect against the threat of heresy was provide both an enlargement and clarification of the ancient creed.[63]

Though documented sources are scarce for the apostles' creed, Hippolytus' *On the Apostolic Tradition*, an early third-century document, hints at the ancient roots of the creed.[64] According to Hippolytus of Rome (AD 170-235), when someone was going to be baptized, they were asked whether they first believed in

---

62 "Apostles' Creed." *Christian Reformed Church.* Accessed June 07, 2018. https://www.crcna.org/welcome/beliefs/creeds/apostles-creed

63 Myers, *The Apostles' Creed*, 3.

64 Ibid.

"God the Father Almighty," then secondly, whether they believed in "Christ Jesus, the Son of God," and thirdly, if they believed in the "Holy Spirit, the holy church, and the resurrection of the saints."[65] This baptistic creed is strikingly similar to what we now recite as the apostles' creed, and is affirmed by church historian Philip Schaff as the "catechumenate" of the early church preceding baptism.[66]

The bishop Irenaeus of Lyons (AD 130-202) adds further weight to an early Christology in his witness of the threefold canon which defined the faith of early Christians:

> The Church, though dispersed through out the whole world, even to the ends of the earth, has received from the apostles and their disciples this faith: [She believes] in one God, the Father Almighty, Maker of heaven, and earth, and the sea, and all things that are in them; and in one Christ Jesus, the Son of God, who became incarnate for our salvation; and in the Holy Spirit, who proclaimed through the prophets... the advents, and the birth from a virgin, and the passion, and the resurrection from the dead, and the ascension into heaven in the flesh of

---

65 See Hippolytus, *On the Apostolic Tradition*, trans. by Alistair Stewart-Sykes (Yonkers, NY.: St. Vladimir's Seminary Press, 2001), 133-136.

66 Philip Schaff, *History of the Christian Church, Vol. II: Ante-Nicene Christianity* (Grand Rapids, MI.: Wm. B. Eerdmans Publishing Company, 1973 [orig. 1910]), 256.

the beloved Christ Jesus, our Lord, and His [future] manifestation from heaven in the glory of the Father 'to gather all things in one,' and to raise up anew all flesh of the whole human race, in order that to Christ Jesus, our Lord, and God, and Saviour, and King, according to the will of the invisible Father, 'every knee should bow, of things in heaven, and things in earth, and things under the earth, and that every tongue should confess' to Him, and that He should execute just judgment towards all… As I have already observed, the Church, having received this preaching and this faith, although scattered throughout the whole world, yet, as if occupying but one house, carefully preserves it. She also believes these points [of doctrine] just as if she had but one soul, and one and the same heart, and she proclaims them, and teaches them, and hands them down, with perfect harmony, as if she possessed only one mouth. For, although the languages of the world are dissimilar, yet the import of the tradition is one and the same.[67]

The creed can thus be better understood as the early "grassroots confession" of the Christian faith, as expressed, for example, by Irenaeus. Scholar Ben Myers writes that it was an "indigenous form of the ancient church's response to the risen Christ, who commanded his apostles to 'make disciples of all nations, baptizing

---

67   Irenaeus of Lyons, "Against the Heresies 1.10.1-2." *Early Christian Writings.* Accessed May 30, 2018. http://www.earlychristianwritings. com/text/irenaeus-book1.html

them in the name of the Father and of the Son and of the Holy Spirit" (Matt. 28:19-20).[68] This ancient catechism served two functions, in its first instance it was instructional, formulaic for memorization and inculcation, and secondly, it was sacramental, used as part of the baptistic rite. On the one hand it is Christian teaching, on the other, a solemn pledge of allegiance. [69] In regards to its Christological content, Schaff writes that the doctrine of Jesus Christ as the God-man and Redeemer served as the "kernel" of all baptismal creeds, for it was "stamped" on the entirety of church life and worship, "expressly asserted" by the church fathers against heresies, "professed" in regular worship and annual celebrations, and ultimately "embodied" in all the prayers and doxologies of the saints.[70] As Schaff affirms, "From the earliest record Christ was the object not of admiration… but of prayer, praise and adoration which is due only to an infinite, uncreated, divine being."[71]

0.5 Pre-Nicene Evidence: Early Church Patristics

But the apostolic creed, together with the text of the New Testament and the extra-biblical witness of pagans, are not the only pre-Nicene evidences for the consensus of early Christology. The teaching of the church patristics should also be considered, given that they

---

68 Myers, *The Apostles' Creed,* 2-3.

69 Ibid, 4-5.

70 Schaff, *History of the Christian Church,* Vol. II, 545

71 Ibid.

were the leaders of the church following the apostles. Ignatius of Antioch (AD 35-108), for example, expressed in his letters a "strong faith and overwhelming love of Christ," what scholar Bruce Metzger regards as "one of the finest literary expressions of Christianity" in the late first and early second century.[72] In fact, Ignatius, bishop of Antioch, wrote his letters in apologetic fashion, addressing the heresy of Gnosticism which was becoming an increased threat to the creed of the early church. Gnosticism, the result of a synthesis between ancient Greek philosophy and Christian theology, according to Haykin, is the belief that "the incarnation of Christ, and consequently his death and resurrection, did not really take place."[73] This is because, as per the Platonic view of the metaphysical, the world is divided into two levels, the matter-form scheme. Both the matter and the forms cannot be reconciled, therefore, Christ the perfect one could not have truly manifested himself in the flesh because the material is imperfect and resistant to formation.

It is for this reason that Ignatius wrote his letters, to affirm the apostolic teaching of Christ as "God incarnate," revealing himself as the person of God in the flesh of man.[74] He is the *Logos*, the Word, made flesh,

---

72 Cited in John E. Lawyer, Jr., "Eucharist and Martyrdom in the Letters of Ignatius of Antioch," *Anglican Theological Review* 73 (1991): 281.

73 Haykin, *The Church Fathers*, 14.

74 Cited in Ibid, 14.

the only- and beloved-begotten Son. There is no mistaking Ignatius' theology, his letters make clear that he believes Jesus to be God, and not having been created before creation, but abiding "with the Father before the beginning of time."[75] As Haykin concludes, "Ignatius' statement that Jesus was 'with the Father' and John's declaration that the Word 'was with God' are making the same point: Jesus Christ/the Word has enjoyed an intimate, personal communion with the Father that is eternal in nature."[76]

Polycarp (AD 69-155), bishop of Smyrna and disciple of the apostle John according to the testimony of Irenaeus, wrote in his *Letter to the Philippians* that Christians are to "believe in our Lord God Jesus Christ and in his Father who raised him from the dead."[77] Justin Martyr (AD 100-165), a Christian apologist, wrote in his *First Apology* that "The Father of the universe has a Son; who also, being the first-begotten Word of God, is even God."[78] Clement of Alexandria (AD 150-215) wrote in his *Exhortation to the Heathen* that "This Word,

75 Ignatius, "Letter to the Magnesians 6." *New Advent.* Trans. by Alexander Roberts and James Donaldson. Accessed June 02, 2018. http://www.newadvent.org/fathers/0105.htm

76 Haykin, *The Church Fathers*, 15.

77 Polycarp, "Philippians, 12:2." *New Advent.* Trans. by Alexander Roberts and James Donaldson. Accessed June 02, 2018. http://www.newadvent.org/fathers/0136.htm

78 Justin Martyr, "First Apology, 63." *Logos Library.* Trans. by Alexander Roberts and James Donaldson. Accessed June 02, 2018. http://www.logoslibrary.org/justin/apology1/63.html

then, the Christ, the cause of both our being at first (for He was in God) and of our well-being, this very Word has now appeared as man, He alone being both, both God and man."[79] And Tertullian (AD 150-225), another early apologist, wrote in his *Treatise on the Soul* that "For God alone is without sin; and the only man without sin is Christ, since Christ is also God."[80] He is God eternal, forever pre-existent, for he testifies that "the Father, and the Son, and the Spirit are inseparable from each other."[81]

We can even turn to the *Letter to Diognetus*, an anonymous work penned sometime in the second century AD,[82] from one who is seeking to persuade a "Graeco-Roman pagan by the name of Diognetus to make a... commitment to the Christian faith."[83] The high Christology, similar to the other patristical writings, is embodied in the text, reflective of the pre-Nicene consensus:

---

79 Clement of Alexandria, "Exhortation to the Heathen, 1." *New Advent*. Trans. by William Wilson. Accessed June 02, 2018. http://www.newadvent.org/fathers/020801.htm

80 Tertullian, "Treatise on the Soul, 41." *New Advent*. Trans. by Peter Holmes. Accessed June 02, 2018. http://www.newadvent.org/fathers/0310.htm

81 Tertullian, "Against Praxeas, 9." *New Advent*. Trans. by Peter Holmes. Accessed June 02, 2018. http://www.newadvent.org/fathers/0317.htm

82 Robert M. Grant, *Greek Apologists of the Second Century* (Philadelphia: Westminster Press, 1988), 178-179.

83 Haykin, *The Church Fathers*, 15.

[Jesus] is the One by whom all things have been set in order, determined, and placed in subjection – both the heavens and things in the heavens, the earth and things on the earth, the sea and the things in the sea, fire, air, abyss, the things in the heights and those in the depths and the realm between. Such was the One God sent to them. …In gentleness and meekness he sent him, as a King sending his son who is a king. He sent him as God, he sent him as [man] to men, he sent him as Savior.[84]

There are several other writings by the early patristics that affirm the Christology of Jesus; and though the church would certainly wrestle with the specifics of Christ's person in relation to the Father and the nature of his deity, the consensus was that Jesus is God, uncreated and eternally begotten. It cannot be denied that there is an element of mystery to this, for as created beings we have a limited, finite understanding of reality, and in particular, of the eternal and infinite.

0.6 The Implications of *Homoousios* and *Homoiousios*

It may have already become evident that the Arian controversy deals with more than just the nature and identity of the Son, it extends to the deity of the Holy Spirit, and calls into question the constitution of the Holy Trinity, and the nature of the incarnation, central doctrines to

---

84 *Letter to Diognetus* 7.2.4. cited in Ibid.

Christian revelation.[85] As I had earlier recorded, in AD 350, the Arian sect of the Anomians stressed the term *anomoios* for the Son, which meant completely "unlike," in reaction to Arius' initial use of the term *homoios*, which meant "like" the Father. Basil of Ancyra proposed *homoiousios* as a middle ground to appease the Arians, which meant the Son's similarity of essence with the Father, and this became the agreed to term for the Arian movement. But the implications of adopting *homoiousios* to describe the Son results in the unintended break-up of Christian theology, something that Arius appears to have wilfully ignored. This is why the Nicene council chose, as a majority, to maintain the *homoousios* of the Son, that being of "one divine essence or substance as the Father," and as a result preserved the harmony and integrity of Christian theology by remaining faithful to the clear teaching of Scripture.[86]

This was not something new in the life and ministry of the church, instead it was a novel articulation of that which always was in the teaching of the church, or perhaps it could be said, a more specific articulation of the Father, Son and Spirit being of "one in essence, or consubstantial. They are in one another, inseparable, and cannot be conceived without each other" as Schaff puts

---

85   Philip Schaff, *History of the Christian Church*, Vol. III: Nicene and Post-Nicene Christianity (Grand Rapids, MI.: Wm. B. Eerdmans, 1974 [orig. 1910]), 618.

86   Ibid., 672.

it.[87] In its literal sense, *Homoousios* means, not numerical identity, but the equality in essence. Thus, the church does not teach belief in God as one being *and* three persons, but rather God as one being *in* three persons, a "solidaric unity."[88]

Arius wouldn't see God in this way, however. No matter how many interchanges he had with various patristics, he held to what was the kernel of Arian doctrine, that Jesus is not equal, nor is he of one essence with the Father. The church, according to Arius, worships the Father "as without beginning because of Him who in time has come to be. And adore Him as everlasting, because of Him who in time has come to be."[89] Athanasius rightly took issue with this, it contradicted the apostolic teaching of the Son, for while the New Testament taught in its simplicity the unity of the Father, Son and Spirit, Arius emerged on the scene thinking that the rest of the church had been distorting the Scriptures for three-to-four centuries. To him, the Son does not even know his own essence, "for, being Son, He really existed, at the will of the Father."[90] He taught that God the Father is alone self-subsistent (Gk. *Agennetos*), immaterial, and thus without any plurality in his being. And that by the will of God, the Son was brought forth into being, as a "perfect creature," just not

---

87 Schaff, *History of the Christian Church*, 672.

88 Ibid.

89 Cited in Leithart, *Athanasius*, 3.

90 Cited in Ibid., 4.

"one among others."[91] Thus, it can be said, faithful to Arianism, that God was not always a father, there was a time when he had no Son.[92] But can it then be said that God is immutable? Does his being not change, not being a Father, and later becoming a Father? What about his attributes, such as his love and relationality? Can God be loving and relational if before time there was no one whom he could love and be relational with? This would render God incapable of love and relationality. As the scholar Donald MacLeod writes, "[W]ithout [the eternal sonship] we lose our measure of the divine love… without the eternal sonship the Trinity becomes inaccessible and incomprehensible."[93] This is not a problem that plagues biblical theology; within the triune Godhead, the Father, Son and Spirit express love for one another and are relational with each other. By their distinctive properties we can distinguish "one person from another" within the Godhead.[94] Arianism, however, encounters severe complications, principle of which is the blurring of the Creator-creation distinction.

No matter how one might try to work it, the monistic direction of Arian theology leads to either of two planes, the first is that creation is elevated to godhood, sufficient to say that creation can be considered divine.

---

91 Williams, *Arius*, 98.

92 Ibid., 100.

93 Donald MacLeod, *The Person of Christ: Contours of Christian Theology* (Downers Grove, IL.: InterVarsity Press, 1998), 128-129.

94 Ibid., 129.

Arius would have denied this, but then that leaves the other plane, God is reduced to the level of the creature. This too would have been denied by Arius, hence why Jesus is not fully in essence man, but nor is he of essence God. He cannot, however, escape the inevitable monistic direction, for Jesus being a creature is admittedly worshiped, and this would reduce Arians to idolatry, worshiping the creature rather than the Creator.[95] This monistic direction is the inevitable result of blurring the Creator-creation distinction, for as Leithart affirms, Athanasius' main thrust in his polemics was that "the Arian theology of 'total otherness' collapses into a pantheistic monism."[96]

0.7 The Epistemological Error

The monistic structure and direction of Arianism is reflective of the very sinister intent underlying the theological system, that being, the preservation of man's pretended "autonomy." It has always been the natural man's desire, since the fall, to be independent of God existentially, epistemologically, and morally. As opposed to being under God's creational —and revealed— law, man sought to reinvent his world and life, positing a different narrative, a different reality, where man could serve as the measure of all things. It is true that the pagans worshiped false gods, but behind those gods, it was man who was worshiped, for it was man who

---

95 Leithart, *Athanasius*, 23.
96 Ibid., 2.

acted as judge to determine what "gods" existed, how they ought to be worshipped and how their lives were to reflect this invented reality. The word "autonomy" comes from two Greek words, *auto* for "self" and *nomos* for "law." In other words, "self law," to be a law unto oneself, a stark contrast to being under God's law. The apologist Greg L. Bahnsen put it this way:

> "Autonomy" refers to being a law unto oneself, so that one's thinking is independent of any outside authority, including God's. Autonomous reasoning takes itself philosophically as the final point of reference and interpretation, the ultimate court of intellectual appeal; it presumes to be self-governing, self-determinative, and self-directing.[97]

The epistemological difference between Athanasius and Arius is that, Athanasius heeded God's scriptural revelation as his ultimate authority for all knowledge, that is to say, as the final point of reference and interpretation, while Arius substituted the inspired word with himself as the ultimate court of intellectual appeal. As opposed to adopting the clear teaching of Scripture, the very same presuppositions of God's word, he imposed upon it his pagan understanding rooted in ancient Greek philosophy, and therefore read into the sacred text his own perversion of the truth. Athanasius approached the word of God with a renewed mind in Christ, having been

---

97   Greg L. Bahnsen, *Van Til's Apologetic: Readings & Analysis* (Phillipsburg, NJ.: P&R Publishing, 1998), 1.

regenerated by the Spirit of God, but Arius approached with a fallen and apostate mind, imposing pagan philosophy, bent on repressing God's truth and in maintaining man's "pretended" autonomy.

Arianism can, in fact, be shown to be closely related to the Aristotelic school in regards to its philosophical approach, where the logical system is to primarily "baffle an adversary," as per 19th century scholar John Henry Newman, "or at most to detect error, rather than to establish truth."[98] The relationship, however, goes beyond its model of inquiry and debate and is rooted in the fact that Arians and other "leaders of the heretical body" were taught by Sophists, Greek philosophical teachers, who acknowledged Aristotle as their principal authority.[99] Arius' art of disputation is that of a Sophist, other Arians such as Asterius of Petra (who later renounced Arianism) was a Sophist by profession, Aetius of Antioch was taught in the School of an Aristotelian of Alexandria, and Eunomius, student of Aetius, known for reconstructing Arian doctrine at the end of the reign of Constantius, is likewise an Aristotelian.[100] This understanding of Arian origins is supported by the writings of Gregory of Nazianzus (c. 276-374), Gregory of Nyssa (c. 335-395), Basil of Caesarea (c. 329-379), Ambrose of Milan (c. 340-397), and Cyril of Jerusalem (c.

---

98 John Henry Newman, *The Arians of the Fourth Century* (USA: Assumption Press, 2004 [orig. 1833]), 19.

99 Ibid.

100 Ibid., 19-20.

313-386), all of whom express Aristotle as "the Bishop of the Arians."[101]

The Greek philosophical roots of Arian thought thus sheds light on its articulation of the Father and the Son, for it explains the structure and direction of Arius' "questions of usage, metaphor and genre in his exegesis."[102] He perceived chaos in the portrayal of the mediator between God and creation in God's word and sought to bring order by developing a supposedly biblical and "rationally consistent catechesis."[103] It is like attempting to explain the relation of the perfect with the imperfect, the world of forms with the world of matter, following the Greek matter-form scheme. However, in spite of presenting himself as the defender of traditional orthodoxy, he revealed himself all the more as a deviant from orthodox theology, and in particular, Christology.[104] He was not informed primarily by the text of Scripture, but his own rationalism, the radical autonomy typical of Aristotelianism. This is why it has been difficult for historians to identify him with a certain "theological school," he is a different breed of a theologian, synthesizing Greek philosophical presuppositions with biblical theology, producing in the end an idolatrous religion.[105] For by denying the deity of the Son, and either elevating

---

101 Ibid., 20.
102 Williams, *Arius*, 111.
103 Ibid.
104 Ibid., 115.
105 Ibid.

the creature to the level of the Creator, or reducing the Creator to the level of the creature, man is presented as equal in some form, but not in nature or essence. He can be, though under the guise of religious worship of another, his own god. It is of no wonder then that Arian theology was so popular with the masses, it catered to their fallen desire to be like God in a way unbefitting for a creature.

0.8 Conclusion

In conclusion, Brown's *DaVinci Code* is nothing more than fiction as to its accusation of Constantine's manipulation of the church creed to deify Christ. If a case were to be made for Constantine's meddling, or the emperors who followed, it would have been for the imposition of Arian theology as opposed to traditional orthodoxy. How many times, for example, was Athanasius exiled because he refused to yield? And though the masses were swayed by Arianism, the majority of the patristics were following Athanasius' lead. Had Athanasius yielded to the emperor's demands, it would have been a devastating blow to the resistance movement of the patristics. Athanasius, however, remained faithful under persecution, and the church fathers followed, condemning Arius well beyond the Nicene council of AD 325.

It is also demonstrable by the New Testament text that the apostles held to Jesus as being God the Son, co-eternal, and consubstantial with the Father. Given that these texts pre-date the fourth century council at

Nicaea, it serves as evidence that Arianism was the novel theology, not the other way around. Put that together with the *Carmen Christi*, that being the first century church hymn, the testimony of pagan sources and then the latter testimony of the pre-Nicene church fathers, and it proves impossible to assert that similar accusations like Brown's are sustainable. It becomes nothing more than baseless conspiracy theories, not taking into account historical facts. Therefore, over against the idea of St. Athanasius or the Nicene council as the fabricators of a Christological Christianity, that is, the holy faith centred around and built upon the God-man Jesus Christ, the patristic of the 4th century AD and his later allies at the council defended *orthodox* Christology which pre-dated the fourth century. They are, what one might call, heroes of the true faith.

May we follow suit and take up the banner of biblical truth in our day and age, for we are living in a time where we need men and women with the spirit of Athanasius, willing to preserve and advance God's truth in a confused and fallen world, living lives worthy of the titular moniker *Contra Mundum* for the glory of God.

Icon of St. Athanasius, Patriarch of Alexandria,
Saint and Doctor of the Church

On the Incarnation

St. Athanasius

1.0 Editor's Note

THE FOLLOWING ENGLISH TRANSLATION of St. Athanasius' "On the Incarnation" was realized by Philip Schaff, D.D., LL.D. (1819-1893), who served as Professor of Church History in the Union Theological Seminary of New York. He also oversaw the translation of "Athanasius: Select Works and Letters" as part of the *Select Library of the Nicene and Post-Nicene Fathers of the Christian Church*. Schaff's translations of St. Athanasius' works are available in the public domain.

While the original text of the translation manuscript has been preserved, small edits have been made to better facilitate the reading experience. For example, though the original text of the chapter headers has been maintained, changes were made to the numbering of the headers for simplicity of reference. In regard to Scriptural citations, the same wording as the original translation has likewise been maintained, however footnotes have been added with Scriptural source references. In addition, some footnote comments have also been added by the editor where deemed necessary for clarity, and paragraph breaks have been introduced in cases where paragraphs were running longer than a full page. We trust you will enjoy reading this timeless masterpiece which has impacted the witness of the church throughout the ages.

Soli Deo Gloria

1.1 Creation and the Fall

1.1.1 In our former book[1] we dealt fully enough with a few of the chief points about the heathen worship of idols, and how those false fears originally arose. We also, by God's grace, briefly indicated that the Word of the Father is Himself divine, that all things that are owe their being to His will and power, and that it is through Him that the Father gives order to creation, by Him that all things are moved, and through Him that they receive their being. Now, Macarius,[2] true lover of Christ, we must take a step further in the faith of our holy religion, and consider also the Word's becoming Man and His divine Appearing in our midst. That mystery the Jews traduce, the Greeks deride, but we adore; and your own love and devotion to the Word also will be the greater, because in His Manhood He seems so little worth. For it is a fact that the more unbelievers pour scorn on Him, so much the more does He make His Godhead evident. The things which they, as men, rule out as impossible, He plainly shows to be possible; that which they deride as unfitting, His goodness makes most fit; and things

---

1   See St. Athanasius, *Contra Gentes [Against the Heathens]*

2   Believed to be Macarius of Jerusalem (ca. 335), served as Bishop of Jerusalem from AD 312-335.

which these wiseacres laugh at as "human" He by His inherent might declares divine. Thus, by what seems His utter poverty and weakness on the cross He overturns the pomp and parade of idols, and quietly and hiddenly wins over the mockers and unbelievers to recognize Him as God.

Now in dealing with these matters it is necessary first to recall what has already been said. You must understand why it is that the Word of the Father, so great and so high, has been made manifest in bodily form. He has not assumed a body as proper to His own nature, far from it, for as the Word He is without body. He has been manifested in a human body for this reason only, out of the love and goodness of His Father, for the salvation of us men. We will begin, then, with the creation of the world and with God its Maker, for the first fact that you must grasp is this: the renewal of creation has been wrought by the Self-same Word Who made it in the beginning. There is thus no inconsistency between creation and salvation for the One Father has employed the same Agent for both works, effecting the salvation of the world through the same Word Who made it in the beginning.

1.1.2 In regard to the making of the universe and the creation of all things there have been various opinions, and each person has propounded the theory that suited his own taste. For instance, some say that all things are self-originated and, so to speak, haphazard. The Epicureans are among these; they deny that there is any

Mind behind the universe at all. This view is contrary to all the facts of experience, their own existence included. For if all things had come into being in this automatic fashion, instead of being the outcome of Mind, though they existed, they would all be uniform and without distinction. In the universe everything would be sun or moon or whatever it was, and in the human body the whole would be hand or eye or foot. But in point of fact the sun and the moon and the earth are all different things, and even within the human body there are different members, such as foot and hand and head. This distinctness of things argues not a spontaneous generation but a prevenient Cause; and from that Cause we can apprehend God, the Designer and Maker of all.

Others take the view expressed by Plato, that giant among the Greeks. He said that God had made all things out of pre-existent and uncreated matter, just as the carpenter makes things only out of wood that already exists. But those who hold this view do not realize that to deny that God is Himself the Cause of matter is to impute limitation to Him, just as it is undoubtedly a limitation on the part of the carpenter that he can make nothing unless he has the wood. How could God be called Maker and Artificer if His ability to make depended on some other cause, namely on matter itself? If He only worked up existing matter and did not Himself bring matter into being, He would be not the Creator but only a craftsman.

Then, again, there is the theory of the Gnostics, who have invented for themselves an Artificer of all things other than the Father of our Lord Jesus Christ. These simply shut their eyes to the obvious meaning of Scripture. For instance, the Lord, having reminded the Jews of the statement in Genesis, "He Who created them in the beginning made them male and female…," and having shown that for that reason a man should leave his parents and cleave to his wife, goes on to say with reference to the Creator, "What therefore God has joined together, let no man put asunder."[3] How can they get a creation independent of the Father out of that? And, again, St. John, speaking all inclusively, says, "All things became by Him and without Him came nothing into being."[4] How then could the Artificer be someone different, other than the Father of Christ?

1.1.3 Such are the notions which men put forward. But the impiety of their foolish talk is plainly declared by the divine teaching of the Christian faith. From it we know that, because there is Mind behind the universe, it did not originate itself; because God is infinite, not finite, it was not made from pre-existent matter, but out of nothing and out of non-existence absolute and utter God brought it into being through the Word. He says as much in Genesis: "In the beginning God created the heavens and the earth;[5] and again through that most

---

3 Matthew 19:4-6
4 John 1:3
5 Genesis 1:1

helpful book The Shepherd, "Believe thou first and foremost that there is One God Who created and arranged all things and brought them out of non-existence into being."[6] Paul also indicates the same thing when he says, "By faith we understand that the worlds were framed by the Word of God, so that the things which we see now did not come into being out of things which had previously appeared."[7] For God is good—or rather, of all goodness He is Fountainhead, and it is impossible for one who is good to be mean or grudging about anything. Grudging existence to none therefore, He made all things out of nothing through His own Word, our Lord Jesus Christ and of all these His earthly creatures He reserved especial mercy for the race of men. Upon them, therefore, upon men who, as animals, were essentially impermanent, He bestowed a grace which other creatures lacked – namely the impress of His own Image, a share in the reasonable being of the very Word Himself, so that, reflecting Him and themselves becoming reasonable and expressing the Mind of God even as He does, though in limited degree they might continue for ever in the blessed and only true life of the saints in paradise. But since the will of man could turn either way, God secured this grace that He had given by making it conditional from the first upon two things – namely, a law and a place.

---

6 The Shepherd of Hermas, Book II, I.
7 Hebrews 11:3

He set them in His own paradise, and laid upon them a single prohibition. If they guarded the grace and retained the loveliness of their original innocence, then the life of paradise should be theirs, without sorrow, pain or care, and after it the assurance of immortality in heaven. But if they went astray and became vile, throwing away their birthright of beauty, then they would come under the natural law of death and live no longer in paradise, but, dying outside of it, continue in death and in corruption. This is what Holy Scripture tells us, proclaiming the command of God, "Of every tree that is in the garden thou shalt surely eat, but of the tree of the knowledge of good and evil ye shall not eat, but in the day that ye do eat, ye shall surely die."[8] "Ye shall surely die" – not just die only, but remain in the state of death and of corruption.

1.1.4 You may be wondering why we are discussing the origin of men when we set out to talk about the Word's becoming Man. The former subject is relevant to the latter for this reason: it was our sorry case that caused the Word to come down, our transgression that called out His love for us, so that He made haste to help us and to appear among us. It is we who were the cause of His taking human form, and for our salvation that in His great love He was both born and manifested in a human body. For God had made man thus (that is, as an embodied spirit), and had willed that he should

---

8 Genesis 2:16f

remain in incorruption. But men, having turned from the contemplation of God to evil of their own devising, had come inevitably under the law of death. Instead of remaining in the state in which God had created them, they were in process of becoming corrupted entirely, and death had them completely under its dominion.

For the transgression of the commandment was making them turn back again according to their nature; and as they had at the beginning come into being out of non-existence, so were they now on the way to returning, through corruption, to non-existence again. The presence and love of the Word had called them into being; inevitably, therefore when they lost the knowledge of God, they lost existence with it; for it is God alone Who exists, evil is non-being, the negation and antithesis of good. By nature, of course, man is mortal, since he was made from nothing; but he bears also the Likeness of Him Who is, and if he preserves that Likeness through constant contemplation, then his nature is deprived of its power and he remains incorrupt. So is it affirmed in Wisdom: "The keeping of His laws is the assurance of incorruption."[9] And being incorrupt, he would be henceforth as God, as Holy Scripture says, "I have said, Ye are gods and sons of the Highest all of you: but ye die as men and fall as one of the princes."[10]

---

9 Wisdom 6:18
10 Psalm 82:6f

1.1.5 This, then, was the plight of men. God had not only made them out of nothing, but had also graciously bestowed on them His own life by the grace of the Word. Then, turning from eternal things to things corruptible, by counsel of the devil, they had become the cause of their own corruption in death; for, as I said before, though they were by nature subject to corruption, the grace of their union with the Word made them capable of escaping from the natural law, provided that they retained the beauty of innocence with which they were created. That is to say, the presence of the Word with them shielded them even from natural corruption, as also Wisdom says: "God created man for incorruption and as an image of His own eternity; but by envy of the devil death entered into the world."[11] When this happened, men began to die, and corruption ran riot among them and held sway over them to an even more than natural degree, because it was the penalty of which God had forewarned them for transgressing the commandment. Indeed, they had in their sinning surpassed all limits; for, having invented wickedness in the beginning and so involved themselves in death and corruption, they had gone on gradually from bad to worse, not stopping at any one kind of evil, but continually, as with insatiable appetite, devising new kinds of sins. Adulteries and thefts were everywhere, murder and raping filled the earth, law was disregarded in corruption and injustice, all kinds of iniquities were perpetrated by all, both singly

11 Wisdom 2:23f

and in common. Cities were warring with cities, nations were rising against nations, and the whole earth was rent with factions and battles, while each strove to outdo the other in wickedness. Even crimes contrary to nature were not unknown, but as the martyr-apostle of Christ says: "Their women changed the natural use into that which is against nature; and the men also, leaving the natural use of the woman, flamed out in lust towards each other, perpetrating shameless acts with their own sex, and receiving in their own persons the due recompense of their pervertedness."[12]

1.2 The Divine Dilemma and its Solution in the Incarnation

1.2.6 We saw in the last chapter that, because death and corruption were gaining ever firmer hold on them, the human race was in process of destruction. Man, who was created in God's image and in his possession of reason reflected the very Word Himself, was disappearing, and the work of God was being undone. The law of death, which followed from the Transgression, prevailed upon us, and from it there was no escape. The thing that was happening was in truth both monstrous and unfitting. It would, of course, have been unthinkable that God should go back upon His word and that man, having transgressed, should not die; but it was equally monstrous that beings which once had shared the nature of the Word should perish and turn back again into

---

12   Romans 1:26f

non-existence through corruption. It was unworthy of the goodness of God that creatures made by Him should be brought to nothing through the deceit wrought upon man by the devil; and it was supremely unfitting that the work of God in mankind should disappear, either through their own negligence or through the deceit of evil spirits. As, then, the creatures whom He had created reasonable, like the Word, were in fact perishing, and such noble works were on the road to ruin, what then was God, being Good, to do? Was He to let corruption and death have their way with them? In that case, what was the use of having made them in the beginning? Surely it would have been better never to have been created at all than, having been created, to be neglected and perish; and, besides that, such indifference to the ruin of His own work before His very eyes would argue not goodness in God but limitation, and that far more than if He had never created men at all. It was impossible, therefore, that God should leave man to be carried off by corruption, because it would be unfitting and unworthy of Himself.

1.2.7 Yet, true though this is, it is not the whole matter. As we have already noted, it was unthinkable that God, the Father of Truth, should go back upon His word regarding death in order to ensure our continued existence. He could not falsify Himself; what, then, was God to do? Was He to demand repentance from men for their transgression? You might say that that was worthy of God, and argue further that, as through the

Transgression they became subject to corruption, so through repentance they might return to incorruption again. But repentance would not guard the Divine consistency, for, if death did not hold dominion over men, God would still remain untrue. Nor does repentance recall men from what is according to their nature; all that it does is to make them cease from sinning. Had it been a case of a trespass only, and not of a subsequent corruption, repentance would have been well enough; but when once transgression had begun men came under the power of the corruption proper to their nature and were bereft of the grace which belonged to them as creatures in the Image of God. No, repentance could not meet the case. What – or rather Who was it that was needed for such grace and such recall as we required? Who, save the Word of God Himself, Who also in the beginning had made all things out of nothing? His part it was, and His alone, both to bring again the corruptible to incorruption and to maintain for the Father His consistency of character with all. For He alone, being Word of the Father and above all, was in consequence both able to recreate all, and worthy to suffer on behalf of all and to be an ambassador for all with the Father.

1.2.8 For this purpose, then, the incorporeal and incorruptible and immaterial Word of God entered our world. In one sense, indeed, He was not far from it before, for no part of creation had ever been without Him Who, while ever abiding in union with the Father, yet fills all things that are. But now He entered the world in a new way, stooping to our level in His love and Self-revealing to us. He saw the reasonable race, the race of men that, like Himself, expressed the Father's Mind, wasting out of existence, and death reigning over all in corruption. He saw that corruption held us all the closer, because it was the penalty for the Transgression; He saw, too, how unthinkable it would be for the law to be repealed before it was fulfilled. He saw how unseemly it was that the very things of which He Himself was the Artificer should be disappearing. He saw how the surpassing wickedness of men was mounting up against them; He saw also their universal liability to death. All this He saw and, pitying our race, moved with compassion for our limitation, unable to endure that death should have the mastery, rather than that His creatures should perish and the work of His Father for us men come to nought, He took to Himself a body, a human body even as our own. Nor did He will merely to become embodied or merely to appear; had that been so, He could have revealed His divine majesty in some other and better way. No, He took our body, and not only so, but He took it directly from a spotless, stainless virgin, without the agency of human father – a pure body, untainted by intercourse with man. He, the Mighty One, the Artificer of all, Himself prepared this body in the virgin as a temple for Himself, and took it for His very own, as the instrument through which He was known and in which He dwelt. Thus, taking a body like our own, because all our bodies were liable to the corruption of death, He surrendered

His body to death instead of all, and offered it to the Father. This He did out of sheer love for us, so that in His death all might die, and the law of death thereby be abolished because, having fulfilled in His body that for which it was appointed, it was thereafter voided of its power for men. This He did that He might turn again to incorruption men who had turned back to corruption, and make them alive through death by the appropriation of His body and by the grace of His resurrection. Thus, He would make death to disappear from them as utterly as straw from fire.

1.2.9 The Word perceived that corruption could not be got rid of otherwise than through death; yet He Himself, as the Word, being immortal and the Father's Son, was such as could not die. For this reason, therefore, He assumed a body capable of death, in order that it, through belonging to the Word Who is above all, might become in dying a sufficient exchange for all, and, itself remaining incorruptible through His indwelling, might thereafter put an end to corruption for all others as well, by the grace of the resurrection. It was by surrendering to death the body which He had taken, as an offering and sacrifice free from every stain, that He forthwith abolished death for His human brethren by the offering of the equivalent. For naturally, since the Word of God was above all, when He offered His own temple and bodily instrument as a substitute for the life of all, He fulfilled in death all that was required. Naturally also, through this union of the immortal Son of God with our human nature, all men were clothed with incorruption in the promise of the resurrection. For the solidarity of mankind is such that, by virtue of the Word's indwelling in a single human body, the corruption which goes with death has lost its power over all. You know how it is when some great king enters a large city and dwells in one of its houses; because of his dwelling in that single house, the whole city is honoured, and enemies and robbers cease to molest it. Even so is it with the King of all; He has come into our country and dwelt in one body amidst the many, and in consequence the designs of the enemy against mankind have been foiled and the corruption of death, which formerly held them in its power, has simply ceased to be. For the human race would have perished utterly had not the Lord and Saviour of all, the Son of God, come among us to put an end to death.

1.2.10 This great work was, indeed, supremely worthy of the goodness of God. A king who has founded a city, so far from neglecting it when through the carelessness of the inhabitants it is attacked by robbers, avenges it and saves it from destruction, having regard rather to his own honour than to the people's neglect. Much more, then, the Word of the All-good Father was not unmindful of the human race that He had called to be; but rather, by the offering of His own body He abolished the death which they had incurred, and corrected their neglect by His own teaching. Thus, by His own power He restored the whole nature of man. The Saviour's own inspired disciples assure us of this. We read in one place: "For the love of Christ constraineth us, because we thus judge that, if One died on behalf of all, then all died, and He died for all that we should no longer live unto ourselves, but unto Him who died and rose again from the dead, even our Lord Jesus Christ."[13]

And again, another says: "But we behold Him Who hath been made a little lower than the angels, even Jesus, because of the suffering of death crowned with glory and honour, that by the grace of God He should taste of death on behalf of every man." The same writer goes on to point out why it was necessary for God the Word and none other to become Man: "For it became Him, for Whom are all things and through Whom are all things, in bringing many sons unto glory, to make the Author of their salvation perfect through suffering."[14] He means that the rescue of mankind from corruption was the proper part only of Him Who made them in the beginning. He points out also that the Word assumed a human body, expressly in order that He might offer it in sacrifice for other like bodies: "Since then the children are sharers in flesh and blood, He also Himself assumed the same, in order that through death He might bring to nought Him that hath the power of death, that is to say, the Devil, and might rescue those who all their lives were enslaved by the fear of death."[15] For by the sacrifice of His own body He did two things: He put an end to

13 2 Corinthians 5:14f
14 Hebrews 2:9ff
15 Hebrews 2:14f

the law of death which barred our way; and He made a new beginning of life for us, by giving us the hope of resurrection. By man death has gained its power over men; by the Word made Man death has been destroyed and life raised up anew. That is what Paul says, that true servant of Christ: "For since by man came death, by man came also the resurrection of the dead. Just as in Adam all die, even so in Christ shall all be made alive,"[16] and so forth. Now, therefore, when we die we no longer do so as men condemned to death, but as those who are even now in process of rising we await the general resurrection of all, "which in its own times He shall show,"[17] even God Who wrought it and bestowed it on us.

This, then, is the first cause of the Saviour's becoming Man. There are, however, other things which show how wholly fitting is His blessed presence in our midst; and these we must now go on to consider.

1.3 The Divine Dilemma and its Solution in the Incarnation (Continued)

1.3.11 When God the Almighty was making mankind through His own Word, He perceived that they, owing to the limitation of their nature, could not of themselves have any knowledge of their Artificer, the Incorporeal and Uncreated. He took pity on them, therefore, and did not leave them destitute of the knowledge of Himself, lest their very existence should prove purposeless. For of

16 1 Corinthians 15:21f
17 1 Timothy 6:15

what use is existence to the creature if it cannot know its Maker? How could men be reasonable beings if they had no knowledge of the Word and Reason of the Father, through Whom they had received their being? They would be no better than the beasts, had they no knowledge save of earthly things; and why should God have made them at all, if He had not intended them to know Him? But, in fact, the good God has given them a share in His own Image, that is, in our Lord Jesus Christ, and has made even themselves after the same Image and Likeness. Why? Simply in order that through this gift of Godlikeness in themselves they may be able to perceive the Image Absolute, that is the Word Himself, and through Him to apprehend the Father; which knowledge of their Maker is for men the only really happy and blessed life.

But, as we have already seen, men, foolish as they are, thought little of the grace they had received, and turned away from God. They defiled their own soul so completely that they not only lost their apprehension of God, but invented for themselves other gods of various kinds. They fashioned idols for themselves in place of the truth and reverenced things that are not, rather than God Who is, as St. Paul says, "worshipping the creature rather than the Creator."[18] Moreover, and much worse, they transferred the honour which is due to God to material objects such as wood and stone, and also to

---

18 Romans 1:25

man; and further even than that they went, as we said in our former book. Indeed, so impious were they that they worshipped evil spirits as gods in satisfaction of their lusts. They sacrificed brute beasts and immolated men, as the just due of these deities, thereby bringing themselves more and more under their insane control. Magic arts also were taught among them, oracles in sundry places led men astray, and the cause of everything in human life was traced to the stars as though nothing existed but that which could be seen. In a word, impiety and lawlessness were everywhere, and neither God nor His Word was known. Yet He had not hidden Himself from the sight of men nor given the knowledge of Himself in one way only; but rather He had unfolded it in many forms and by many ways.

1.3.12 God knew the limitation of mankind, you see; and though the grace of being made in His Image was sufficient to give them knowledge of the Word and through Him of the Father, as a safeguard against their neglect of this grace, He provided the works of creation also as means by which the Maker might be known. Nor was this all. Man's neglect of the indwelling grace tends ever to increase; and against this further frailty also God made provision by giving them a law, and by sending prophets, men whom they knew. Thus, if they were tardy in looking up to heaven, they might still gain knowledge of their Maker from those close at hand; for men can learn directly about higher things from other men. Three ways thus lay open to them, by which they might obtain the knowledge of God. They could look up into the immensity of heaven, and by pondering the harmony of creation come to know its Ruler, the Word of the Father, Whose all-ruling providence makes known the Father to all. Or, if this was beyond them, they could converse with holy men, and through them learn to know God, the Artificer of all things, the Father of Christ, and to recognize the worship of idols as the negation of the truth and full of all impiety. Or else, in the third place, they could cease from lukewarmness and lead a good life merely by knowing the law. For the law was not given only for the Jews, nor was it solely for their sake that God sent the prophets, though it was to the Jews that they were sent and by the Jews that they were persecuted. The law and the prophets were a sacred school of the knowledge of God and the conduct of the spiritual life for the whole world.

So great, indeed, were the goodness and the love of God. Yet men, bowed down by the pleasures of the moment and by the frauds and illusions of the evil spirits, did not lift up their heads towards the truth. So burdened were they with their wickednesses that they seemed rather to be brute beasts than reasonable men, reflecting the very Likeness of the Word.

1.3.13 What was God to do in face of this dehumanising of mankind, this universal hiding of the knowledge of Himself by the wiles of evil spirits? Was He to keep silence before so great a wrong and let men go on being thus deceived and kept in ignorance of Himself? If so, what was the use of having made them in His own Image originally? It would surely have been better for them always to have been brutes, rather than to revert to that condition when once they had shared the nature of the Word. Again, things being as they were, what was the use of their ever having had the knowledge of God? Surely it would have been better for God never to have bestowed it, than that men should subsequently be found unworthy to receive it. Similarly, what possible profit could it be to God Himself, Who made men, if when made they did not worship Him, but regarded others as their makers? This would be tantamount to His having made them for others and not for Himself. Even an earthly king, though he is only a man, does not allow lands that he has colonized to pass into other hands or to desert to other rulers, but sends letters and friends and even visits them himself to recall them to their allegiance, rather than allow His work to be undone. How much more, then, will God be patient and painstaking with His creatures, that they be not led astray from Him to the service of those that are not, and that all the more because such error means for them sheer ruin, and because it is not right that those who had once shared His Image should be destroyed.

What, then, was God to do? What else could He possibly do, being God, but renew His Image in mankind, so that through it men might once more come to know Him? And how could this be done save by the coming of the very Image Himself, our Saviour Jesus

Christ? Men could not have done it, for they are only made after the Image; nor could angels have done it, for they are not the images of God. The Word of God came in His own Person, because it was He alone, the Image of the Father Who could recreate man made after the Image.

In order to effect this re-creation, however, He had first to do away with death and corruption. Therefore He assumed a human body, in order that in it death might once for all be destroyed, and that men might be renewed according to the Image. The Image of the Father only was sufficient for this need. Here is an illustration to prove it.

1.3.14 You know what happens when a portrait that has been painted on a panel becomes obliterated through external stains. The artist does not throw away the panel, but the subject of the portrait has to come and sit for it again, and then the likeness is re-drawn on the same material. Even so was it with the All-holy Son of God. He, the Image of the Father, came and dwelt in our midst, in order that He might renew mankind made after Himself, and seek out His lost sheep, even as He says in the Gospel: "I came to seek and to save that which was lost."[19] This also explains His saying to the Jews: "Except a man be born anew…"[20] as He was not referring to a man's natural birth from his mother, as

---

19 Luke 19:10
20 John 3:3

they thought, but to the re-birth and re-creation of the soul in the Image of God.

Nor was this the only thing which only the Word could do. When the madness of idolatry and irreligion filled the world and the knowledge of God was hidden, whose part was it to teach the world about the Father? Man's, would you say? But men cannot run everywhere over the world, nor would their words carry sufficient weight if they did, nor would they be, unaided, a match for the evil spirits. Moreover, since even the best of men were confused and blinded by evil, how could they convert the souls and minds of others? You cannot put straight in others what is warped in yourself. Perhaps you will say, then, that creation was enough to teach men about the Father. But if that had been so, such great evils would never have occurred. Creation was there all the time, but it did not prevent men from wallowing in error. Once more, then, it was the Word of God, Who sees all that is in man and moves all things in creation, Who alone could meet the needs of the situation. It was His part and His alone, Whose ordering of the universe reveals the Father, to renew the same teaching. But how was He to do it? By the same means as before, perhaps you will say, that is, through the works of creation. But this was proven insufficient. Men had neglected to consider the heavens before, and now they were looking in the opposite direction. Wherefore, in all naturalness and fitness, desiring to do good to men, as Man He dwells, taking to Himself a body like the rest; and through His actions done in that body, as it were on their own level, He teaches those who would not learn by other means to know Himself, the Word of God, and through Him the Father.

1.3.15 He deals with them as a good teacher with his pupils, coming down to their level and using simple means. St. Paul says as much: "Because in the wisdom of God the world in its wisdom knew not God, God thought fit through the simplicity of the News proclaimed to save those who believe."[21] Men had turned from the contemplation of God above, and were looking for Him in the opposite direction, down among created things and things of sense. The Saviour of us all, the Word of God, in His great love took to Himself a body and moved as Man among men, meeting their senses, so to speak, half way. He became Himself an object for the senses, so that those who were seeking God in sensible things might apprehend the Father through the works which He, the Word of God, did in the body. Human and human minded as men were, therefore, to whichever side they looked in the sensible world they found themselves taught the truth. Were they awe-stricken by creation? They beheld it confessing Christ as Lord. Did their minds tend to regard men as Gods? The uniqueness of the Saviour's works marked Him, alone of men, as Son of God. Were they drawn to evil spirits? They saw them driven out by the Lord and learned that the Word

---

21   1 Corinthians 1:21

of God alone was God and that the evil spirits were not gods at all. Were they inclined to hero-worship and the cult of the dead? Then the fact that the Saviour had risen from the dead showed them how false these other deities were, and that the Word of the Father is the one true Lord, the Lord even of death. For this reason was He both born and manifested as Man, for this He died and rose, in order that, eclipsing by His works all other human deeds, He might recall men from all the paths of error to know the Father. As He says Himself, "I came to seek and to save that which was lost."[22]

1.3.16 When, then, the minds of men had fallen finally to the level of sensible things, the Word submitted to appear in a body, in order that He, as Man, might center their senses on Himself, and convince them through His human acts that He Himself is not man only but also God, the Word and Wisdom of the true God. This is what Paul wants to tell us when he says: "That ye, being rooted and grounded in love, may be strong to apprehend with all the saints what is the length and breadth and height and depth, and to know the love of God that surpasses knowledge, so that ye may be filled unto all the fullness of God."[23]

The Self-revealing of the Word is in every dimension – above, in creation; below, in the Incarnation; in the depth, in Hades; in the breadth, throughout the world.

---

22 Luke 19:10
23 Ephesians 3:17ff

All things have been filled with the knowledge of God. For this reason He did not offer the sacrifice on behalf of all immediately He came, for if He had surrendered His body to death and then raised it again at once He would have ceased to be an object of our senses. Instead of that, He stayed in His body and let Himself be seen in it, doing acts and giving signs which showed Him to be not only man, but also God the Word. There were thus two things which the Saviour did for us by becoming Man. He banished death from us and made us anew; and, invisible and imperceptible as in Himself He is, He became visible through His works and revealed Himself as the Word of the Father, the Ruler and King of the whole creation.

1.3.17 There is a paradox in this last statement which we must now examine. The Word was not hedged in by His body, nor did His presence in the body prevent His being present elsewhere as well. When He moved His body He did not cease also to direct the universe by His Mind and might. No. The marvelous truth is, that being the Word, so far from being Himself contained by anything, He actually contained all things Himself. In creation He is present everywhere, yet is distinct in being from it; ordering, directing, giving life to all, containing all, yet is He Himself the Uncontained, existing solely in His Father. As with the whole, so also is it with the part. Existing in a human body, to which He Himself gives life, He is still Source of life to all the universe, present in every part of it, yet outside the whole; and He is revealed both through the works of His body and through His activity in the world. It is, indeed, the function of soul to behold things that are outside the body, but it cannot energize or move them. A man cannot transport things from one place to another, for instance, merely by thinking about them; nor can you or I move the sun and the stars just by sitting at home and looking at them. With the Word of God in His human nature, however, it was otherwise. His body was for Him not a limitation, but an instrument, so that He was both in it and in all things, and outside all things, resting in the Father alone. At one and the same time – this is the wonder – as Man He was living a human life, and as Word He was sustaining the life of the universe, and as Son He was in constant union with the Father. Not even His birth from a virgin, therefore, changed Him in any way, nor was He defiled by being in the body. Rather, He sanctified the body by being in it. For His being in everything does not mean that He shares the nature of everything, only that He gives all things their being and sustains them in it. Just as the sun is not defiled by the contact of its rays with earthly objects, but rather enlightens and purifies them, so He Who made the sun is not defiled by being made known in a body, but rather the body is cleansed and quickened by His indwelling, "Who did no sin, neither was guile found in His mouth."[24]

---

24 1 Peter 2:22

1.3.18 You must understand, therefore, that when writers on this sacred theme speak of Him as eating and drinking and being born, they mean that the body, as a body, was born and sustained with the food proper to its nature; while God the Word, Who was united with it, was at the same time ordering the universe and revealing Himself through His bodily acts as not man only but God. Those acts are rightly said to be His acts, because the body which did them did indeed belong to Him and none other; moreover, it was right that they should be thus attributed to Him as Man, in order to show that His body was a real one and not merely an appearance. From such ordinary acts as being born and taking food, He was recognized as being actually present in the body; but by the extraordinary acts which He did through the body He proved Himself to be the Son of God. That is the meaning of His words to the unbelieving Jews: "If I do not the works of My Father, believe Me not; but if I do, even if ye believe not Me, believe My works, that ye may know that the Father is in Me and I in the Father."[25]

Invisible in Himself, He is known from the works of creation; so also, when His Godhead is veiled in human nature, His bodily acts still declare Him to be not man only, but the Power and Word of God. To speak authoritatively to evil spirits, for instance, and to drive them out, is not human but divine; and who could see Him curing all the diseases to which mankind is prone, and

---

25   John 10:37-38

still deem Him mere man and not also God? He cleansed lepers, He made the lame to walk, He opened the ears of the deaf and the eyes of the blind, there was no sickness or weakness that He did not drive away. Even the most casual observer can see that these were acts of God. The healing of the man born blind, for instance, who but the Father and Artificer of man, the Controller of his whole being, could thus have restored the faculty denied at birth? He Who did thus must surely be Himself the Lord of birth. This is proved also at the outset of His becoming Man. He formed His own body from the virgin; and that is no small proof of His Godhead, since He Who made that was the Maker of all else. And would not anyone infer from the fact of that body being begotten of a virgin only, without human father, that He Who appeared in it was also the Maker and Lord of all beside?

Again, consider the miracle at Cana. Would not anyone who saw the substance of water transmuted into wine understand that He Who did it was the Lord and Maker of the water that He changed? It was for the same reason that He walked on the sea as on dry land – to prove to the onlookers that He had mastery over all. And the feeding of the multitude, when He made little into much, so that from five loaves five thousand mouths were filled – did not that prove Him none other than the very Lord Whose Mind is over all?

1.4 The Death of Christ

1.4.19 All these things the Saviour thought fit to do, so that, recognizing His bodily acts as works of God, men who were blind to His presence in creation might regain knowledge of the Father. For, as I said before, who that saw His authority over evil spirits and their response to it could doubt that He was, indeed, the Son, the Wisdom and the Power of God? Even the very creation broke silence at His behest and, marvelous to relate, confessed with one voice before the cross, that monument of victory, that He Who suffered thereon in the body was not man only, but Son of God and Saviour of all. The sun veiled his face, the earth quaked, the mountains were rent asunder, all men were stricken with awe. These things showed that Christ on the cross was God, and that all creation was His slave and was bearing witness by its fear to the presence of its Master.

Thus, then, God the Word revealed Himself to men through His works. We must next consider the end of His earthly life and the nature of His bodily death. This is, indeed, the very center of our faith, and everywhere you hear men speak of it; by it, too, no less than by His other acts, Christ is revealed as God and Son of God.

1.4.20 We have dealt as far as circumstances and our own understanding permit with the reason for His bodily manifestation. We have seen that to change the corruptible to incorruption was proper to none other than the Saviour Himself, Who in the beginning made all things out of nothing; that only the Image of the Father could re-create the likeness of the Image in men, that none save our Lord Jesus Christ could give to mortals immortality, and that only the Word Who orders all things and is alone the Father's true and sole-begotten Son could teach men about Him and abolish the worship of idols. But beyond all this, there was a debt owing which must needs be paid; for, as I said before, all men were due to die. Here, then, is the second reason why the Word dwelt among us, namely that having proved His Godhead by His works, He might offer the sacrifice on behalf of all, surrendering His own temple to death in place of all, to settle man's account with death and free him from the primal transgression. In the same act also He showed Himself mightier than death, displaying His own body incorruptible as the first fruits of the resurrection.

You must not be surprised if we repeat ourselves in dealing with this subject. We are speaking of the good pleasure of God and of the things which He in His loving wisdom thought fit to do, and it is better to put the same thing in several ways than to run the risk of leaving something out. The body of the Word, then, being a real human body, in spite of its having been uniquely formed from a virgin, was of itself mortal and, like other bodies, liable to death. But the indwelling of the Word loosed it from this natural liability, so that corruption could not touch it. Thus, it happened that two opposite marvels took place at once: the death of all was consummated in the Lord's body; yet, because the Word was in it, death and corruption were in the same act utterly abolished. Death there had to be, and death for all, so that the due of all might be paid. Wherefore, the Word, as I said, being Himself incapable of death, assumed a mortal body, that He might offer it as His own in place of all, and suffering for the sake of all through His union with it, "might bring to nought Him that had the power of death, that is, the devil, and might deliver them who all their lifetime were enslaved by the fear of death."[26]

1.4.21 Have no fears then. Now that the common Saviour of all has died on our behalf, we who believe in Christ no longer die, as men died aforetime, in fulfillment of the threat of the law. That condemnation has come to an end; and now that, by the grace of the resurrection, corruption has been banished and done away, we are loosed from our mortal bodies in God's good time for each, so that we may obtain thereby a better resurrection. Like seeds cast into the earth, we do not perish in our dissolution, but like them shall rise again, death having been brought to nought by the grace of the Saviour. That is why blessed Paul, through whom we all have surety of the resurrection, says: "This corruptible must put on incorruption and this mortal must put on immortality; but when this corruptible shall have put on incorruption and this mortal shall

---

26   Hebrews 2:14f

have put on immortality, then shall be brought to pass the saying that is written, 'Death is swallowed up in victory. O Death, where is thy sting? O Grave, where is thy victory?'"[27]

"Well then," some people may say, "if the essential thing was that He should surrender His body to death in place of all, why did He not do so as Man privately, without going to the length of public crucifixion? Surely it would have been more suitable for Him to have laid aside His body with honour than to endure so shameful a death." But look at this argument closely, and see how merely human it is, whereas what the Saviour did was truly divine and worthy of His Godhead for several reasons. The first is this. The death of men under ordinary circumstances is the result of their natural weakness. They are essentially impermanent, so after a time they fall ill and when worn out they die. But the Lord is not like that. He is not weak, He is the Power of God and Word of God and Very Life Itself. If He had died quietly in His bed like other men it would have looked as if He did so in accordance with His nature, and as though He was indeed no more than other men. But because He was Himself Word and Life and Power His body was made strong, and because the death had to be accomplished, He took the occasion of perfecting His sacrifice not from Himself, but from others. How could He fall sick, Who had healed others? Or how could that body weaken and

---

fail by means of which others are made strong? Here, again, you may say, "Why did He not prevent death, as He did sickness?" Because it was precisely in order to be able to die that He had taken a body, and to prevent the death would have been to impede the resurrection. And as to the unsuitability of sickness for His body, as arguing weakness, you may say, "Did He then not hunger?" Yes, He hungered, because that was the property of His body, but He did not die of hunger because He Whose body hungered was the Lord. Similarly, though He died to ransom all, He did not see corruption. His body rose in perfect soundness, for it was the body of none other than the Life Himself.

1.4.22 Someone else might say, perhaps, that it would have been better for the Lord to have avoided the designs of the Jews against Him, and so to have guarded His body from death altogether. But see how unfitting this also would have been for Him. Just as it would not have been fitting for Him to give His body to death by His own hand, being Word and being Life, so also it was not consonant with Himself that He should avoid the death inflicted by others. Rather, He pursued it to the uttermost, and in pursuance of His nature neither laid aside His body of His own accord nor escaped the plotting Jews. And this action showed no limitation or weakness in the Word; for He both waited for death in order to make an end of it, and hastened to accomplish it as an offering on behalf of all. Moreover, as it was the death of all mankind that the Saviour came to accomplish, not

His own, He did not lay aside His body by an individual act of dying, for to Him, as Life, this simply did not belong; but He accepted death at the hands of men, thereby completely to destroy it in His own body.

There are some further considerations which enable one to understand why the Lord's body had such an end. The supreme object of His coming was to bring about the resurrection of the body. This was to be the monument to His victory over death, the assurance to all that He had Himself conquered corruption and that their own bodies also would eventually be incorrupt; and it was in token of that and as a pledge of the future resurrection that He kept His body incorrupt. But there again, if His body had fallen sick and the Word had left it in that condition, how unfitting it would have been! Should He Who healed the bodies of others neglect to keep His own in health? How would His miracles of healing be believed, if this were so? Surely people would either laugh at Him as unable to dispel disease or else consider Him lacking in proper human feeling because He could do so, but did not.

1.4.23 Then, again, suppose without any illness He had just concealed His body somewhere, and then suddenly reappeared and said that He had risen from the dead. He would have been regarded merely as a teller of tales, and because there was no witness of His death, nobody would believe His resurrection. Death had to precede resurrection, for there could be no resurrection without it. A secret and unwitnessed death would have left the resurrection without any proof or evidence to support it. Again, why should He die a secret death, when He proclaimed the fact of His rising openly? Why should He drive out evil spirits and heal the man blind from birth and change water into wine, all publicly, in order to convince men that He was the Word, and not also declare publicly that incorruptibility of His mortal body, so that He might Himself be believed to be the Life? And how could His disciples have had boldness in speaking of the resurrection unless they could state it as a fact that He had first died? Or how could their hearers be expected to believe their assertion, unless they themselves also had witnessed His death? For if the Pharisees at the time refused to believe and forced others to deny also, though the things had happened before their very eyes, how many excuses for unbelief would they have contrived, if it had taken place secretly? Or how could the end of death and the victory over it have been declared, had not the Lord thus challenged it before the sight of all, and by the incorruption of His body proved that henceforward it was annulled and void?

1.4.24 There are some other possible objections that must be answered. Some might urge that, even granting the necessity of a public death for subsequent belief in the resurrection, it would surely have been better for Him to have arranged an honourable death for Himself, and so to have avoided the ignominy of the cross. But even this would have given ground for suspicion that His power over death was limited to the particular kind of death which He chose for Himself; and that again would furnish excuse for disbelieving the resurrection. Death came to His body, therefore, not from Himself but from enemy action, in order that the Saviour might utterly abolish death in whatever form they offered it to Him. A generous wrestler, virile and strong, does not himself choose his antagonists, lest it should be thought that of some of them he is afraid. Rather, he lets the spectators choose them, and that all the more of these are hostile, so that he may overthrow whomsoever they match against him and thus vindicate his superior strength. Even so was it with Christ. He, the Life of all, our Lord and Saviour, did not arrange the manner of his own death lest He should seem to be afraid of some other kind. No. He accepted and bore upon the cross a death inflicted by others, and those others His special enemies, a death which to them was supremely terrible and by no means to be faced; and He did this in order that, by destroying even this death, He might Himself be believed to be the Life, and the power of death be recognized as finally annulled. A marvelous and mighty paradox has thus occurred, for the death which they thought to inflict on Him as dishonour and disgrace has become the glorious monument to death's defeat. Therefore it is also, that He neither endured the death of John, who was beheaded, nor was He sawn asunder, like Isaiah: even in death He preserved His body whole and undivided, so that there should be no excuse hereafter for those who would divide the Church.

1.4.25 So much for the objections of those outside the Church. But if any honest Christian wants to know why He suffered death on the cross and not in some other way, we answer thus: in no other way was it expedient for us, indeed the Lord offered for our sakes the one death that was supremely good. He had come to bear the curse that lay on us; and how could He "become a curse"[28] otherwise than by accepting the accursed death? And that death is the cross, for it is written "Cursed is every one that hangeth on tree."[29] Again, the death of the Lord is the ransom of all, and by it "the middle wall of partition"[30] is broken down and the call of the Gentiles comes about. How could He have called us if He had not been crucified, for it is only on the cross that a man dies with arms outstretched? Here, again, we see the fitness of His death and of those outstretched arms: it was that He might draw His ancient people with the one and the Gentiles with the other, and join both together in Himself. Even so, He foretold the manner of His redeeming death, "I, if I be lifted up, will draw all men unto Myself."[31] Again, the air is the sphere of the devil, the enemy of our race who, having fallen from heaven, endeavors with the other evil spirits who shared in his disobedience both to keep souls from the truth and to hinder the progress of those who are trying to follow

---

28 Galatians 3:13
29 Galatians 3:13
30 Ephesians 2:14
31 John 12:32

it. The apostle refers to this when he says, "According to the prince of the power of the air, of the spirit that now worketh in the sons of disobedience."[32] But the Lord came to overthrow the devil and to purify the air and to make "a way" for us up to heaven, as the apostle says, "through the veil, that is to say, His flesh."[33] This had to be done through death, and by what other kind of death could it be done, save by a death in the air, that is, on the cross? Here, again, you see how right and natural it was that the Lord should suffer thus; for being thus "lifted up," He cleansed the air from all the evil influences of the enemy. "I beheld Satan as lightning falling,"[34] He says; and thus He re-opened the road to heaven, saying again, "Lift up your gates, O ye princes, and be ye lift up, ye everlasting doors."[35] For it was not the Word Himself Who needed an opening of the gates, He being Lord of all, nor was any of His works closed to their Maker. No, it was we who needed it, we whom He Himself upbore in His own body – that body which He first offered to death on behalf of all, and then made through it a path to heaven.

1.5 The Resurrection

1.5.26 Fitting indeed, then, and wholly consonant was the death on the cross for us; and we can see how

---

32 Ephesians 2:2
33 Hebrews 10:20
34 Luke 10:18
35 Psalm 24:7

reasonable it was, and why it is that the salvation of the world could be accomplished in no other way. Even on the cross He did not hide Himself from sight; rather, He made all creation witness to the presence of its Maker. Then, having once let it be seen that it was truly dead, He did not allow that temple of His body to linger long, but forthwith on the third day raised it up, impassable and incorruptible, the pledge and token of His victory.

It was, of course, within His power thus to have raised His body and displayed it as alive directly after death. But the all-wise Saviour did not do this, lest some should deny that it had really or completely died. Besides this, had the interval between His death and resurrection been but two days, the glory of His incorruption might not have appeared. He waited one whole day to show that His body was really dead, and then on the third day showed it incorruptible to all. The interval was no longer, lest people should have forgotten about it and grown doubtful whether it were in truth the same body. No, while the affair was still ringing in their ears and their eyes were still straining and their minds in turmoil, and while those who had put Him to death were still on the spot and themselves witnessing to the fact of it, the Son of God after three days showed His once dead body immortal and incorruptible; and it was evident to all that it was from no natural weakness that the body which the Word indwelt had died, but in order that in it by the Saviour's power death might be done away.

1.5.27 A very strong proof of this destruction of death and its conquest by the cross is supplied by a present fact, namely this. All the disciples of Christ despise death; they take the offensive against it and, instead of fearing it, by the sign of the cross and by faith in Christ trample on it as on something dead. Before the divine sojourn of the Saviour, even the holiest of men were afraid of death, and mourned the dead as those who perish. But now that the Saviour has raised His body, death is no longer terrible, but all those who believe in Christ tread it underfoot as nothing, and prefer to die rather than to deny their faith in Christ, knowing full well that when they die they do not perish, but live indeed, and become incorruptible through the resurrection. But that devil who of old wickedly exulted in death, now that the pains of death are loosed, he alone it is who remains truly dead. There is proof of this too; for men who, before they believe in Christ, think death horrible and are afraid of it, once they are converted despise it so completely that they go eagerly to meet it, and themselves become witnesses of the Saviour's resurrection from it. Even children hasten thus to die, and not men only, but women train themselves by bodily discipline to meet it. So weak has death become that even women, who used to be taken in by it, mock at it now as a dead thing robbed of all its strength. Death has become like a tyrant who has been completely conquered by the legitimate monarch; bound hand and foot the passers-by sneer at him, hitting him and abusing him, no longer afraid of his cruelty and rage, because of the king who has conquered him. So has death been conquered and branded for what it is by the Saviour on the cross. It is bound hand and foot, all who are in Christ trample it as they pass and as witnesses to Him deride it, scoffing and saying, "O Death, where is thy victory? O Grave, where is thy sting?"[36]

1.5.28 Is this a slender proof of the impotence of death, do you think? Or is it a slight indication of the Saviour's victory over it, when boys and young girls who are in Christ look beyond this present life and train themselves to die? Everyone is by nature afraid of death and of bodily dissolution; the marvel of marvels is that he who is enfolded in the faith of the cross despises this natural fear and for the sake of the cross is no longer cowardly in face of it. The natural property of fire is to burn. Suppose, then, that there was a substance such as the Indian asbestos is said to be, which had no fear of being burnt, but rather displayed the impotence of the fire by proving itself unburnable. If anyone doubted the truth of this, all he need do would be to wrap himself up in the substance in question and then touch the fire. Or, again, to revert to our former figure, if anyone wanted to see the tyrant bound and helpless, who used to be such a terror to others, he could do so simply by going into the country of the tyrant's conqueror. Even so, if anyone still doubts the conquest of death, after so many proofs and so many martyrdoms in Christ and

---

36 1 Corinthians 15:55

such daily scorn of death by His truest servants, he certainly does well to marvel at so great a thing, but he must not be obstinate in unbelief and disregard of plain facts. No, he must be like the man who wants to prove the property of the asbestos, and like him who enters the conqueror's dominions to see the tyrant bound. He must embrace the faith of Christ, this disbeliever in the conquest of death, and come to His teaching. Then he will see how impotent death is and how completely conquered. Indeed, there have been many former unbelievers and deriders who, after they became believers, so scorned death as even themselves to become martyrs for Christ's sake.

1.5.29 If, then, it is by the sign of the cross and by faith in Christ that death is trampled underfoot, it is clear that it is Christ Himself and none other Who is the Archvictor over death and has robbed it of its power. Death used to be strong and terrible, but now, since the sojourn of the Saviour and the death and resurrection of His body, it is despised; and obviously it is by the very Christ Who was mounted on the cross, that it has been destroyed and vanquished finally. When the sun rises after the night and the whole world is lit up by it, nobody doubts that it is the sun which has thus shed its light everywhere and driven away the dark. Equally clear is it, since this utter scorning and trampling down of death has ensued upon the Saviour's manifestation in the body and His death on the cross, that it is He Himself Who brought death to nought and daily raises monuments to His victory in His own disciples. How can you think otherwise, when you see men naturally weak hastening to death, unafraid at the prospect of corruption, fearless of the descent into Hades, even indeed with eager soul provoking it, not shrinking from tortures, but preferring thus to rush on death for Christ's sake, rather than to remain in this present life? If you see with your own eyes men and women and children, even, thus welcoming death for the sake of Christ's religion, how can you be so utterly silly and incredulous and maimed in your mind as not to realize that Christ, to Whom these all bear witness, Himself gives the victory to each, making death completely powerless for those who hold His faith and bear the sign of the cross? No one in his senses doubts that a snake is dead when he sees it trampled underfoot, especially when he knows how savage it used to be; nor, if he sees boys making fun of a lion, does he doubt that the brute is either dead or completely bereft of strength. These things can be seen with our own eyes, and it is the same with the conquest of death. Doubt no longer, then, when you see death mocked and scorned by those who believe in Christ, that by Christ death was destroyed, and the corruption that goes with it resolved and brought to end.

1.5.30 What we have said is, indeed, no small proof of the destruction of death and of the fact that the cross of the Lord is the monument to His victory. But the resurrection of the body to immortality, which results henceforward from the work of Christ, the common

Saviour and true Life of all, is more effectively proved by facts than by words to those whose mental vision is sound. For, if, as we have shown, death was destroyed and everybody tramples on it because of Christ, how much more did He Himself first trample and destroy it in His own body! Death having been slain by Him, then, what other issue could there be than the resurrection of His body and its open demonstration as the monument of His victory? How could the destruction of death have been manifested at all, had not the Lord's body been raised? But if anyone finds even this insufficient, let him find proof of what has been said in present facts. Dead men cannot take effective action; their power of influence on others lasts only till the grave. Deeds and actions that energize others belong only to the living.

Well, then, look at the facts in this case. The Saviour is working mightily among men, every day He is invisibly persuading numbers of people all over the world, both within and beyond the Greek-speaking world, to accept His faith and be obedient to His teaching. Can anyone, in face of this, still doubt that He has risen and lives, or rather that He is Himself the Life? Does a dead man prick the consciences of men, so that they throw all the traditions of their fathers to the winds and bow down before the teaching of Christ? If He is no longer active in the world, as He must needs be if He is dead, how is it that He makes the living to cease from their activities, the adulterer from his adultery, the murderer from murdering, the unjust from avarice, while the profane and godless man becomes religious? If He did not rise, but is still dead, how is it that He routs and persecutes and overthrows the false gods, whom unbelievers think to be alive, and the evil spirits whom they worship? For where Christ is named, idolatry is destroyed and the fraud of evil spirits is exposed; indeed, no such spirit can endure that Name, but takes to flight on sound of it. This is the work of One Who lives, not of one dead; and, more than that, it is the work of God. It would be absurd to say that the evil spirits whom He drives out and the idols which He destroys are alive, but that He Who drives out and destroys, and Whom they themselves acknowledge to be Son of God, is dead.

1.5.31 In a word, then, those who disbelieve in the resurrection have no support in facts, if their gods and evil spirits do not drive away the supposedly dead Christ. Rather, it is He Who convicts them of being dead. We are agreed that a dead person can do nothing: yet the Saviour works mightily every day, drawing men to religion, persuading them to virtue, teaching them about immortality, quickening their thirst for heavenly things, revealing the knowledge of the Father, inspiring strength in face of death, manifesting Himself to each, and displacing the irreligion of idols; while the gods and evil spirits of the unbelievers can do none of these things, but rather become dead at Christ's presence, all their ostentation barren and void. By the sign of the cross, on the contrary, all magic is stayed, all sorcery confounded, all the idols are abandoned and deserted, and all senseless pleasure ceases, as the eye of faith looks up from earth to heaven. Whom, then, are we to call dead? Shall we call Christ dead, Who effects all this? But the dead have not the faculty to effect anything. Or shall we call death dead, which effects nothing whatever, but lies as lifeless and ineffective as are the evil spirits and the idols? The Son of God, "living and effective,"[37] is active everyday and effects the salvation of all; but death is daily proved to be stripped of all its strength, and it is the idols and the evil spirits who are dead, not He. No room for doubt remains, therefore, concerning the resurrection of His body.

Indeed, it would seem that he who disbelieves this bodily rising of the Lord is ignorant of the power of the Word and Wisdom of God. If He took a body to Himself at all, and made it His own in pursuance of His purpose, as we have shown that He did, what was the Lord to do with it, and what was ultimately to become of that body upon which the Word had descended? Mortal and offered to death on behalf of all as it was, it could not but die; indeed, it was for that very purpose that the Saviour had prepared it for Himself. But on the other hand, it could not remain dead, because it had become the very temple of Life. It therefore died, as mortal, but lived again because of the Life within it; and its resurrection is made known through its works.

---

37 Hebrews 4:12

1.5.32 It is, indeed, in accordance with the nature of the invisible God that He should be thus known through His works; and those who doubt the Lord's resurrection because they do not now behold Him with their eyes, might as well deny the very laws of nature. They have ground for disbelief when works are lacking; but when the works cry out and prove the fact so clearly, why do they deliberately deny the risen life so manifestly shown? Even if their mental faculties are defective, surely their eyes can give them irrefragable proof of the power and Godhead of Christ. A blind man cannot see the sun, but he knows that it is above the earth from the warmth which it affords; similarly, let those who are still in the blindness of unbelief recognize the Godhead of Christ and the resurrection which He has brought about through His manifested power in others. Obviously He would not be expelling evil spirits and despoiling idols, if He were dead, for the evil spirits would not obey one who was dead. If, on the other hand, the very naming of Him drives them forth, He clearly is not dead; and the more so that the spirits, who perceive things unseen by men, would know if He were so and would refuse to obey Him. But, as a matter of fact, what profane persons doubt, the evil spirits know—namely that He is God; and for that reason they flee from Him and fall at His feet, crying out even as they cried when He was in the body, "We know Thee Who Thou art, the Holy One of God," and, "Ah, what have I in common with Thee, Thou Son of God? I implore Thee, torment me not."[38]

Both from the confession of the evil spirits and from the daily witness of His works, it is manifest, then, and let none presume to doubt it, that the Saviour has raised His own body, and that He is very Son of God, having His being from God as from a Father, Whose Word and Wisdom and Whose Power He is. He it is Who in these latter days assumed a body for the salvation of us all, and taught the world concerning the Father. He it is Who has destroyed death and freely graced us all with incorruption through the promise of the resurrection, having raised His own body as its first-fruits, and displayed it by the sign of the cross as the monument to His victory over death and its corruption.

1.6 Refutation of the Jews

1.6.33 We have dealt thus far with the Incarnation of our Saviour, and have found clear proof of the resurrection of His Body and His victory over death. Let us now go further and investigate the unbelief and the ridicule with which Jews and Gentiles respectively regard these same facts. It seems that in both cases the points at issue are the same, namely the unfittingness or incongruity (as it seems to them) alike of the cross and of the Word's becoming man at all. But we have no hesitation in taking up the argument against these objectors, for the proofs on our side are extremely clear.

---

38 Cf. Luke 4:34 and Mark 5:7

First, then, we will consider the Jews. Their unbelief has its refutation in the Scriptures which even themselves read; for from cover to cover the inspired Book clearly teaches these things both in its entirety and in its actual words. Prophets foretold the marvel of the Virgin and of the Birth from her, saying, "Behold, a virgin shall conceive and bear a son, and they shall call his name 'Emmanuel,' which means 'God is with us.'"[39] And Moses, that truly great one in whose word the Jews trust so implicitly, he also recognized the importance and truth of the matter. He puts it thus: "There shall arise a star from Jacob and a man from Israel, and he shall break in pieces the rulers of Moab."[40] And, again, "How lovely are thy dwellings, O Jacob, thy tents, O Israel! Like woodland valleys they give shade, and like parks by rivers, like tents which the Lord has pitched, like cedar-trees by streams. There shall come forth a Man from among his seed, and he shall rule over many peoples."[41] And, again, Isaiah says, "Before the Babe shall be old enough to call father or mother, he shall take the power of Damascus and the spoils of Samaria from under the eyes of the king of Assyria."[42] These words, then, fore-tell that a Man shall appear. And Scripture proclaims further that He that is to come is Lord of all. These are the words, "Behold, the Lord sitteth on an airy cloud

---

39 Isaiah 7:14

40 Numbers 24:17

41 Numbers 24:5-7

42 Isaiah 8:4

and shall come into Egypt, and the man-made images of Egypt shall be shaken."[43] And it is from Egypt also that the Father calls him back, saying, "Out of Egypt have I called My Son."[44]

1.6.34 Moreover, the Scriptures are not silent even about His death. On the contrary, they refer to it with the utmost clearness. They have not feared to speak also of the cause of it. He endures it, they say, not for His own sake, but for the sake of bringing immortality and salvation to all, and they record also the plotting of the Jews against Him and all the indignities which He suffered at their hands. Certainly nobody who reads the Scriptures can plead ignorance of the facts as an excuse for error! There is this passage, for instance: "A man that is afflicted and knows how to bear weakness, for His face is turned away. He was dishonoured and not considered, He bears our sins and suffers for our sakes. And we for our part thought Him distressed and afflicted and ill-used; but it was for our sins that He was wounded and for our lawlessness that He was made weak. Chastisement for our peace was upon Him, and by His bruising we are healed."[45] O marvel at the love of the Word for men, for it is on our account that He is dishonoured, so that we may be brought to honour. "For all we," it goes on, "have strayed like sheep, man has strayed from his path, and the Lord has given Him up for our sins; and He

---

43   Isaiah 19:1

44   Hosea 11:1

45   Isaiah 53:3-5

Himself did not open His mouth at the ill-treatment. Like a sheep He was led to slaughter, and as a lamb is dumb before its shearer, so He opened not His mouth; in His humiliation His judgment was taken away."[46] And then Scripture anticipates the surmises of any who might think from His suffering thus that He was just an ordinary man, and shows what power worked in His behalf. "Who shall declare of what lineage He comes?" it says, "for His life is exalted from the earth. By the lawlessness of the people was He brought to death, and I will give the wicked in return for His burial and the rich in return for His death. For He did no lawlessness, neither was deceit found in His mouth. And the Lord wills to heal Him of His affliction."[47]

1.6.35 You have heard the prophecy of His death, and now, perhaps, you want to know what indications there are about the cross. Even this is not passed over in silence: on the contrary, the sacred writers proclaim it with the utmost plainness. Moses foretells it first, and that right loudly, when he says, "You shall see your Life hanging before your eyes, and shall not believe."[48] After him the prophets also give their witness, saying, "But I as an innocent lamb brought to be offered was yet ignorant of it. They plotted evil against Me, saying, 'Come, let us cast wood into His bread, and wipe Him out from

---

46   Isaiah 53:6-8
47   Isaiah 53: 8-10
48   Deuteronomy 28:66

the land of the living."[49] And, again, "They pierced My hands and My feet, they counted all My bones, they divided My garments for themselves and cast lots for My clothing."[50] Now a death lifted up that takes place on wood can be none other than the death of the cross; moreover, it is only in that death that the hands and feet are pierced. Besides this, since the Saviour dwelt among men, all nations everywhere have begun to know God; and this too Holy Writings expressly mentions. "There shall be the Root of Jesse," it says, "and he who rises up to rule the nations, on Him nations shall set their hope."[51]

These are just a few things in proof of what has taken place; but indeed all Scripture teems with disproof of Jewish unbelief. For example, which of the righteous men and holy prophets and patriarchs of whom the Divine Scriptures tell ever had his bodily birth from a virgin only? Was not Abel born of Adam, Enoch of Jared, Noah of Lamech, Abraham of Terah, Isaac of Abraham, and Jacob of Isaac? Was not Judah begotten by Jacob and Moses and Aaron by Ameram? Was not Samuel the son of Elkanah, David of Jesse, Solomon of David, Hezekiah of Ahaz, Josiah of Amon, Isaiah of Amos, Jeremiah of Hilkiah and Ezekiel of Buzi? Had not each of these a father as author of his being? So who is He that is born of a virgin only, that sign of which the prophet makes so much? Again, which of all those

49 Jeremiah 11:19
50 Psalm 22:16-18
51 Isaiah 11:10

people had his birth announced to the world by a star in the heavens? When Moses was born his parents hid him. David was unknown even in his own neighborhood, so that mighty Samuel himself was ignorant of his existence and asked whether Jesse had yet another son. Abraham again became known to his neighbors as a great man only after his birth. But with Christ it was otherwise. The witness to His birth was not man, but a star shining in the heavens whence He was coming down.

1.6.36 Then, again, what king that ever was reigned and took trophies from his enemies before he had strength to call father or mother? Was not David thirty years old when he came to the throne and Solomon a grown young man? Did not Joash enter on his reign at the age of seven, and Josiah, some time after him, at about the same age, both of them fully able by that time to call father or mother? Who is there, then, that was reigning and despoiling his enemies almost before he was born? Let the Jews, who have investigated the matter, tell us if there was ever such a king in Israel or Judah—a king upon whom all the nations set their hopes and had peace, instead of being at enmity with him on every side! As long as Jerusalem stood there was constant war between them, and they all fought against Israel. The Assyrians oppressed Israel, the Egyptians persecuted them, the Babylonians fell upon them, and, strange to relate, even the Syrians their neighbors were at war with them. And did not David fight with Moab and smite the Syrians, and Hezekiah quail at the boasting of

Sennacherib? Did not Amalek make war on Moses and the Amorites oppose him, and did not the inhabitants of Jericho array themselves against Joshua the son of Nun? Did not the nations always regard Israel with implacable hostility? Then it is worth inquiring who it is, on whom the nations are to set their hopes. Obviously there must be someone, for the prophet could not have told a lie. But did any of the holy prophets or of the early patriarchs die on the cross for the salvation of all? Was any of them wounded and killed for the healing of all? Did the idols of Egypt fall down before any righteous man or king that came there? Abraham came there certainly, but idolatry prevailed just the same; and Moses was born there, but the mistaken worship was unchanged.

1.6.37 Again, does Scripture tell of anyone who was pierced in hands and feet or hung upon a tree at all, and by means of a cross perfected his sacrifice for the salvation of all? It was not Abraham, for he died in his bed, as did also Isaac and Jacob. Moses and Aaron died in the mountain, and David ended his days in his house, without anybody having plotted against him. Certainly he had been sought by Saul, but he was preserved unharmed. Again Isaiah was sawn asunder, but he was not hung on a tree. Jeremiah was shamefully used, but he did not die under condemnation. Ezekiel suffered, but he did so, not on behalf of the people, but only to signify to them what was going to happen. Moreover, all these even when they suffered were but men, like other men; but He Whom the Scriptures declare to suffer on behalf of all is called not merely man but Life of all, although in point of fact He did share our human nature. "You shall see your Life hanging before your eyes," they say, and "Who shall declare of what lineage He comes?" With all the saints we can trace their descent from the beginning, and see exactly how each came to be; but the Divine Word maintains that we cannot declare the lineage of Him Who is the Life. Who is it, then, of Whom the Holy Writings thus speaks? Who is there so great that even the prophets foretell of Him such mighty things?

There is indeed no one in the Scriptures at all, save the common Saviour of all, the Word of God, our Lord Jesus Christ. He it is that proceeded from a virgin, and appeared as man on earth, He it is Whose earthly lineage cannot be declared, because He alone derives His body from no human father, but from a virgin alone. We can trace the paternal descent of David and Moses and of all the patriarchs. But with the Saviour we cannot do so, for it was He Himself Who caused the star to announce His bodily birth, and it was fitting that the Word, when He came down from heaven, should have His sign in heaven too, and fitting that the King of creation on His coming forth should be visibly recognized by all the world. He was actually born in Judea, yet men from Persia came to worship Him. He it is Who won victory from His demon foes and trophies from the idolaters even before His bodily appearing – namely, all the heathen who from every region have abjured the tradition of their fathers and the false worship of idols and are now placing their hope in Christ and transferring their allegiance to Him. The thing is happening before our very eyes, here in Egypt; and thereby another prophecy is fulfilled, for at no other time have the Egyptians ceased from their false worship save when the Lord of all, riding as on a cloud, came down here in the body and brought the error of idols to nothing and won over everybody to Himself and through Himself to the Father. He it is Who was crucified with the sun and moon as witnesses; and by His death salvation has come to all men, and all creation has been redeemed. He is the Life of all, and He it is Who like a sheep gave up His own body to death, His life for ours and our salvation.

1.6.38 Yet the Jews disbelieve this. This argument does not satisfy them. Well, then, let them be persuaded by other things in their own oracles. Of whom, for instance, do the prophets say "I was made manifest to those who did not seek Me, I was found by those who had not asked for Me? I said, 'See, here am I,' to the nation that had not called upon My Name. I stretched out My hands to a disobedient and gainsaying people."[52] Who is this person that was made manifest, one might ask the Jews?

If the prophet is speaking of himself, then they must tell us how he was first hidden, in order to be manifested afterwards. And, again, what kind of man is this prophet, who was not only revealed after being hidden, but also stretched out his hands upon the cross? Those things

---

52   Isaiah 65:1-2

happened to none of those righteous men: they happened only to the Word of God Who, being by nature without body, on our account appeared in a body and suffered for us all. And if even this is not enough for them, there is other overwhelming evidence by which they may be silenced. The Scripture says, "Be strong, hands that hang down and feeble knees, take courage, you of little faith, be strong and do not fear. See, our God will recompense judgment, He Himself will come and save us. Then the eyes of blind men shall be opened and the ears of deaf men shall hear, and stammerers shall speak distinctly."[53] What can they say to this, or how can they look it in the face at all? For the prophecy does not only declare that God will dwell here, it also makes known the signs and the time of His coming. When God comes, it says, the blind will see, the lame will walk, the deaf will hear and the stammerers will speak distinctly. Can the Jews tell us when such signs occurred in Israel, or when anything of the kind took place at all in Jewry? The leper Naaman was cleansed, it is true, but no deaf man heard nor did any lame man walk. Elijah raised a dead person and so did Elisha; but no one blind from birth received his sight. To raise a dead person is a great thing indeed, but it is not such as the Saviour did. And surely, since the Scriptures have not kept silence about the leper and the dead son of the widow, if a lame man had walked and a blind man had received his sight, they would have mentioned these as well. Their silence

---

53   Isaiah 35:3-6

on these points proves that the events never took place. When therefore did these things happen, unless when the Word of God Himself came in the body? Was it not when He came that lame men walked and stammerers spoke clearly and men blind from birth were given sight? And the Jews who saw it themselves testified to the fact that such things had never before occurred. "Since the world began," they said, "it has never been heard of that anyone should open the eyes of a man born blind. If this Man were not from God, He could do nothing."[54]

1.6.39 But surely they cannot fight against plain facts. So it may be that, without denying what is written, they will maintain that they are still waiting for these things to happen, and that the Word of God is yet to come, for that is a theme on which they are always harping most brazenly, in spite of all the evidence against them. But they shall be refuted on this supreme point more clearly than on any, and that not by ourselves but by the most wise Daniel, for he signifies the actual date of the Saviour's coming as well as His Divine sojourn in our midst. "Seventy weeks," he says, "are cut short upon thy people and upon the holy city, to make a complete end of sin and for sins to be sealed up and iniquities blotted out, and to make reconciliation for iniquity and to seal vision and prophet, and to anoint a Holy One of holies. And thou shalt know and understand

---

54 John 9:32-33

from the going forth of the Word to answer,[55] and to build Jerusalem, until Christ the Prince."[56] In regard to the other prophecies, they may possibly be able to find excuses for deferring their reference to a future time, but what can they say to this one? How can they face it at all? Not only does it expressly mention the Anointed One, that is the Christ, it even declares that He Who is to be anointed is not man only, but the Holy One of holies! And it says that Jerusalem is to stand till His coming, and that after it prophet and vision shall cease in Israel! David was anointed of old, and Solomon, and Hezekiah; but then Jerusalem and the place stood, and prophets were prophesying, Gad and Asaph and Nathan, and later Isaiah and Hosea and Amos and others. Moreover, those men who were anointed were called holy certainly, but none of them was called the Holy of holies. Nor is it any use for the Jews to take refuge in the Captivity, and say that Jerusalem did not exist then, for what about the prophets? It is a fact that at the outset of the Exile Daniel and Jeremiah were there, and Ezekiel and Haggai and Zechariah also prophesied.

1.6.40 So the Jews are indulging in fiction, and transferring present time to future. When did prophet and vision cease from Israel? Was it not when Christ came, the Holy One of holies? It is, in fact, a sign and notable

---

55 "Answer" is a Septuagint (LXX) misreading for the Hebrew word "restore", the Septuagint is an ancient Alexandrian translation of Jewish Scriptures into Koine Greek.

56 Daniel 9:24-25

proof of the coming of the Word that Jerusalem no longer stands, neither is prophet raised up nor vision revealed among them. And it is natural that it should be so, for when He that was signified had come, what need was there any longer of any to signify Him? And when the Truth had come, what further need was there of the shadow? On His account only they prophesied continually, until such time as Essential Righteousness has come, Who was made the Ransom for the sins of all. For the same reason Jerusalem stood until the same time, in order that there men might premeditate the types before the Truth was known. So, of course, once the Holy One of holies had come, both vision and prophecy were sealed. And the kingdom of Jerusalem ceased at the same time, because kings were to be anointed among them only until the Holy of holies had been anointed. Moses also prophesies that the kingdom of the Jews shall stand until His time, saying, "A ruler shall not fail from Judah nor a prince from his loins, until the things laid up for him shall come and the Expectation of the nations Himself."[57]

And that is why the Saviour Himself was always proclaiming "The law and the prophets prophesied until John."[58] So if there is still king or prophet or vision among the Jews, they do well to deny that Christ is come; but if there is neither king nor vision, and since that time all prophecy has been sealed and city and temple taken,

---

57 Genesis 49:10
58 Matthew 11:13

how can they be so irreligious, how can they so flaunt the facts, as to deny Christ Who has brought it all about? Again, they see the heathen forsaking idols and setting their hopes through Christ on the God of Israel; why do they yet deny Christ Who after the flesh was born of the root of Jesse and reigns henceforward? Of course, if the heathen were worshipping some other god, and not confessing the God of Abraham and Isaac and Jacob and Moses, then they would do well to argue that God had not come. But if the heathen are honouring the same God Who gave the law to Moses and the promises to Abraham – the God Whose word too the Jews dishonoured, why do they not recognize or rather why do they deliberately refuse to see that the Lord of Whom the Scriptures prophesied has shone forth to the world and appeared to it in a bodily form? Scripture declares it repeatedly. "The Lord God has appeared to us,"[59] and again, "He sent forth His Word and healed them."[60] And again, "It was no ambassador, no angel who saved us, but the Lord Himself."[61] The Jews are afflicted like some demented person who sees the earth lit up by the sun, but denies the sun that lights it up! What more is there for their Expected One to do when he comes? To call the heathen? But they are called already. To put an end to prophet and king and vision? But this too has already happened. To expose the Goddenyingness of idols? It is

59   Psalm 118:27
60   Psalm 107:20
61   Isaiah 63:9

already exposed and condemned. Or to destroy death? It is already destroyed. What then has not come to pass that the Christ must do? What is there left out or unfulfilled that the Jews should disbelieve so light-heartedly? The plain fact is, as I say, that there is no longer any king or prophet nor Jerusalem nor sacrifice nor vision among them; yet the whole earth is filled with the knowledge of God, and the Gentiles, forsaking atheism, are now taking refuge with the God of Abraham through the Word, our Lord Jesus Christ.

Surely, then, it must be plain even to the most shameless that the Christ has come, and that He has enlightened all men everywhere, and given them the true and divine teaching about His Father. Thus the Jews may be refuted by these and other arguments from the Divine teaching.

1.7 Refutation of the Gentiles

1.7.41 We come now to the unbelief of the Gentiles; and this is indeed a matter for complete astonishment, for they laugh at that which is no fit subject for mockery, yet fail to see the shame and ridiculousness of their own idols. But the arguments on our side do not lack weight, so we will confute them too on reasonable grounds, chiefly from what we ourselves also see.

First of all, what is there in our belief that is unfitting or ridiculous? Is it only that we say that the Word has been manifested in a body? Well, if they themselves really love the truth, they will agree with us that this involved no unfittingness at all. If they deny that there is a Word of God at all, that will be extraordinary, for then they will be ridiculing what they do not know. But suppose they confess that there is a Word of God, that He is the Governor of all things, that in Him the Father wrought the creation, that by His providence the whole receives light and life and being, and that He is King over all, so that He is known by means of the works of His providence, and through Him the Father. Suppose they confess all this, what then? Are they not unknowingly turning the ridicule against themselves? The Greek philosophers say that the universe is a great body, and they say truly, for we perceive the universe and its parts with our senses. But if the Word of God is in the universe, which is a body, and has entered into it in its every part, what is there surprising or unfitting in our saying that He has entered also into human nature? If it were unfitting for Him to have embodied Himself at all, then it would be unfitting for Him to have entered into the universe, and to be giving light and movement by His providence to all things in it, because the universe, as we have seen, is itself a body. But if it is right and fitting for Him to enter into the universe and to reveal Himself through it, then, because humanity is part of the universe along with the rest, it is no less fitting for Him to appear in a human body, and to enlighten and to work through that. And surely if it were wrong for a part of the universe to have been used to reveal His

Divinity to men, it would be much more wrong that He should be so revealed by the whole!

1.7.42 Take a parallel case. A man's personality actuates and quickens his whole body. If anyone said it was unsuitable for the man's power to be in the toe, he would be thought silly, because, while granting that a man penetrates and actuates the whole of his body, he denied his presence in the part. Similarly, no one who admits the presence of the Word of God in the universe as a whole should think it unsuitable for a single human body to be by Him actuated and enlightened.

But is it, perhaps, because humanity is a thing created and brought into being out of non-existence that they regard as unfitting the manifestation of the Saviour in our nature? If so, it is high time that they spurned Him from creation too; for it, too, has been brought out of non-being into being by the Word. But if, on the other hand, although creation is a thing that has been made, it is not unsuitable for the Word to be present in it, then neither is it unsuitable for Him to be in man. Man is a part of the creation, as I said before; and the reasoning which applies to one applies to the other. All things derive from the Word their light and movement and life, as the Gentile authors themselves say, "In Him we live and move and have our being."[62] Very well then. That being so, it is by no means unbecoming that the Word should dwell in man. So if, as we say, the Word has

---

62 See Acts 17:28

used that in which He is as the means of His self-mani-
festation, what is there ridiculous in that? He could not
have used it had He not been present in it; but we have
already admitted that He is present both in the whole
and in the parts. What, then, is there incredible in His
manifesting Himself through that in which He is? By
His own power He enters completely into each and all,
and orders them throughout ungrudgingly; and, had
He so willed, He could have revealed Himself and His
Father by means of sun or moon or sky or earth or fire
or water. Had He done so, no one could rightly have
accused Him of acting unbecomingly, for He sustains in
one whole all things at once, being present and invisibly
revealed not only in the whole, but also in each particular part. This being so, and since, moreover, He has
willed to reveal Himself through men, who are part of
the whole, there can be nothing ridiculous in His using
a human body to manifest the truth and knowledge
of the Father. Does not the mind of man pervade his
entire being, and yet find expression through one part
only, namely the tongue? Does anybody say on that
account that Mind has degraded itself? Of course not.
Very well, then, no more is it degrading for the Word,
Who pervades all things, to have appeared in a human
body. For, as I said before, if it were unfitting for Him
thus to indwell the part, it would be equally so for Him
to exist within the whole.

1.7.43 Some may then ask, why did He not manifest
Himself by means of other and nobler parts of creation,

and use some nobler instrument, such as sun or moon or stars or fire or air, instead of mere man? The answer is this. The Lord did not come to make a display. He came to heal and to teach suffering men. For one who wanted to make a display the thing would have been just to appear and dazzle the beholders. But for Him Who came to heal and to teach the way was not merely to dwell here, but to put Himself at the disposal of those who needed Him, and to be manifested according as they could bear it, not vitiating the value of the Divine appearing by exceeding their capacity to receive it.

Moreover, nothing in creation had erred from the path of God's purpose for it, save only man. Sun, moon, heaven, stars, water, air, none of these had swerved from their order, but, knowing the Word as their Maker and their King, remained as they were made. Men alone having rejected what is good, have invented nothings instead of the truth, and have ascribed the honour due to God and the knowledge concerning Him to demons and men in the form of stones. Obviously the Divine goodness could not overlook so grave a matter as this. But men could not recognize Him as ordering and ruling creation as a whole. So what does He do? He takes to Himself for instrument a part of the whole, namely a human body, and enters into that. Thus, He ensured that men should recognize Him in the part who could not do so in the whole, and that those who could not lift their eyes to His unseen power might recognize and behold Him in the likeness of themselves. For, being men, they would naturally learn to know His Father more quickly and directly by means of a body that corresponded to their own and by the Divine works done through it; for by comparing His works with their own they would judge His to be not human but Divine. And if, as they say, it were unsuitable for the Word to reveal Himself through bodily acts, it would be equally so for Him to do so through the works of the universe. His being in creation does not mean that He shares its nature; on the contrary, all created things partake of His power. Similarly, though He used the body as His instrument, He shared nothing of its defect, but rather sanctified it by His indwelling. Does not even Plato, of whom the Greeks think so much, say that the Author of the Universe, seeing it storm-tossed and in danger of sinking into the state of dissolution, takes his seat at the helm of the Life-force of the universe, and comes to the rescue and puts everything right? What, then, is there incredible in our saying that, mankind having gone astray, the Word descended upon it and was manifest as man, so that by His intrinsic goodness and His steersmanship He might save it from the storm?

1.7.44 It may be, however, that, though shamed into agreeing that this objection is void, the Greeks will want to raise another. They will say that, if God wanted to instruct and save mankind, He might have done so, not by His Word's assumption of a body, but, even as He at first created them, by the mere signification of His will. The reasonable reply to that is that the circumstances in the two cases are quite different. In the beginning, nothing as yet existed at all; all that was needed, therefore, in order to bring all things into being, was that His will to do so should be signified. But once man was in existence, and things that were, not things that were not, demanded to be healed, it followed as a matter of course that the Healer and Saviour should align Himself with those things that existed already, in order to heal the existing evil. For that reason, therefore, He was made man, and used the body as His human instrument. If this were not the fitting way, and He willed to use an instrument at all, how otherwise was the Word to come? And whence could He take His instrument, save from among those already in existence and needing His Godhead through One like themselves? It was not things non-existent that needed salvation, for which a bare creative word might have sufficed, but man – man already in existence and already in process of corruption and ruin. It was natural and right, therefore, for the Word to use a human instrument and by that means unfold Himself to all.

You must know, moreover, that the corruption which had set in was not external to the body but established within it. The need, therefore, was that life should cleave to it in corruption's place, so that, just as death was brought into being in the body, life also might be engendered in it. If death had been exterior to the body, life might fittingly have been the same. But if death was within the body, woven into its very substance and dominating it as though completely one with it, the need was for Life to be woven into it instead, so that the body by thus enduing itself with life might cast corruption off. Suppose the Word had come outside the body instead of in it, He would, of course, have defeated death, because death is powerless against the Life. But the corruption inherent in the body would have remained in it nonetheless. Naturally, therefore, the Saviour assumed a body for Himself, in order that the body, being interwoven as it were with life, should no longer remain a mortal thing, in thrall to death, but as endued with immortality and risen from death, should thenceforth remain immortal. For once having put on corruption, it could not rise, unless it put on life instead; and besides this, death of its very nature could not appear otherwise than in a body. Therefore He put on a body, so that in the body He might find death and blot it out. And, indeed, how could the Lord have been proved to be the Life at all, had He not endued with life that which was subject to death?

Take an illustration. Stubble is a substance naturally destructible by fire; and it still remains stubble, fearing the menace of fire which has the natural property of consuming it, even if fire is kept away from it, so that it is not actually burnt. But suppose that, instead of merely keeping the fire from it somebody soaks the stubble with a quantity of asbestos, the substance which is said to be the antidote to fire. Then the stubble no longer fears the fire, because it has put on that which fire cannot touch, and therefore it is safe. It is just the same with regard to the body and death. Had death been kept from it by a mere command, it would still have remained mortal and corruptible, according to its nature. To prevent this, it put on the incorporeal Word of God, and therefore fears neither death nor corruption anymore, for it is clad with Life as with a garment and in it corruption is clean done away.

1.7.45 The Word of God thus acted consistently in assuming a body and using a human instrument to vitalize the body. He was consistent in working through man to reveal Himself everywhere, as well as through the other parts of His creation, so that nothing was left void of His Divinity and knowledge. For I take up now the point I made before, namely that the Saviour did this in order that He might fill all things everywhere with the knowledge of Himself, just as they are already filled with His presence, even as the Divine Scripture says, "The whole universe was filled with the knowledge of the Lord."[63] If a man looks up to heaven he sees there His ordering; but if he cannot look so high as heaven, but only so far as men, through His works he sees His power, incomparable with human might, and learns from them that He alone among men is God the Word. Or, if a man has gone astray among demons and is in fear of them, he may see this Man drive them out and judge therefrom that He is indeed their Master. Again, if a man has been immersed in the element of water and thinks

---

63 Isaiah 11:9

that it is God – as indeed the Egyptians do worship water – he may see its very nature changed by Him and learn that the Lord is Creator of all. And if a man has gone down even to Hades, and stands awestruck before the heroes who have descended thither, regarding them as gods, still he may see the fact of Christ's resurrection and His victory over death, and reason from it that, of all these, He alone is very Lord and God. For the Lord touched all parts of creation, and freed and undeceived them all from every deceit. As St. Paul says, "Having put off from Himself the principalities and the powers, He triumphed on the cross,"[64] so that no one could possibly be any longer deceived, but everywhere might find the very Word of God. For thus man, enclosed on every side by the works of creation and everywhere – in heaven, in Hades, in men and on the earth, beholding the unfolded Godhead of the Word, is no longer deceived concerning God, but worships Christ alone, and through Him rightly knows the Father.

On these grounds, then, of reason and of principle, we will fairly silence the Gentiles in their turn. But if they think these arguments insufficient to confute them, we will go on in the next chapter to prove our point from facts.

1.8 Refutation of the Gentiles (Continued)

1.8.46 When did people begin to abandon the worship of idols, unless it were since the very Word of God came

---

64 Colossians 2:15

among men? When have oracles ceased and become void of meaning, among the Greeks and everywhere, except since the Saviour has revealed Himself on earth? When did those whom the poets call gods and heroes begin to be adjudged as mere mortals, except when the Lord took the spoils of death and preserved incorruptible the body He had taken, raising it from among the dead? Or when did the deceitfulness and madness of demons fall under contempt, save when the Word, the Power of God, the Master of all these as well, condescended on account of the weakness of mankind and appeared on earth? When did the practice and theory of magic begin to be spurned under foot, if not at the manifestation of the Divine Word to men? In a word, when did the wisdom of the Greeks become foolish, save when the true Wisdom of God revealed Himself on earth? In old times the whole world and every place in it was led astray by the worship of idols, and men thought the idols were the only gods that were. But now all over the world men are forsaking the fear of idols and taking refuge with Christ; and by worshipping Him as God they come through Him to know the Father also, Whom formerly they did not know. The amazing thing, moreover, is this. The objects of worship formerly were varied and countless; each place had its own idol and the so-called god of one place could not pass over to another in order to persuade the people there to worship him, but was barely reverenced even by his own. Indeed no! Nobody worshipped his neighbor's god, but every man had his own idol and thought that it was lord of all. But now Christ alone is worshipped, as One and the Same among all peoples everywhere; and what the feebleness of idols could not do, namely, convince even those dwelling close at hand, He has effected. He has persuaded not only those close at hand, but literally the entire world to worship one and the same Lord and through Him the Father.

1.8.47 Again, in former times every place was full of the fraud of the oracles, and the utterances of those at Delphi and Dordona and in Boeotia and Lycia and Libya and Egypt and those of the Kabiri and the Pythoness were considered marvelous by the minds of men. But now, since Christ has been proclaimed everywhere, their madness too has ceased, and there is no one left among them to give oracles at all. Then, too, demons used to deceive men's minds by taking up their abode in springs or rivers or trees or stones and imposing upon simple people by their frauds. But now, since the Divine appearing of the Word, all this fantasy has ceased, for by the sign of the cross, if a man will but use it, he drives out their deceits. Again, people used to regard as gods those who are mentioned in the poets – Zeus and Kronos and Apollo and the heroes, and in worshipping them they went astray. But now that the Saviour has appeared among men, those others have been exposed as mortal men, and Christ alone is recognized as true God, Word of God, God Himself. And what is one to say about the magic that they think so marvelous? Before the sojourn of the Word, it was strong and active among Egyptians and Chaldeans and Indians and filled all who saw it with terror and astonishment. But by the coming of the Truth and the manifestation of the Word it too has been confuted and entirely destroyed. As to Greek wisdom, however, and the philosophers' noisy talk, I really think no one requires argument from us; for the amazing fact is patent to all that, for all that they had written so much, the Greeks failed to convince even a few from their own neighborhood in regard to immortality and the virtuous ordering of life. Christ alone, using common speech and through the agency of men not clever with their tongues, has convinced whole assemblies of people all the world over to despise death, and to take heed to the things that do not die, to look past the things of time and gaze on things eternal, to think nothing of earthly glory and to aspire only to immortality.

1.8.48 These things which we have said are no mere words: they are attested by actual experience. Anyone who likes may see the proof of glory in the virgins of Christ, and in the young men who practice chastity as part of their religion, and in the assurance of immortality in so great and glad a company of martyrs. Anyone, too, may put what we have said to the proof of experience in another way. In the very presence of the fraud of demons and the imposture of the oracles and the wonders of magic, let him use the sign of the cross which they all mock at, and but speak the Name of Christ, and he shall see how through Him demons are routed, oracles cease, and all magic and witchcraft is confounded.

Who, then, is this Christ and how great is He, Who by His Name and presence overshadows and confounds all things on every side, Who alone is strong against all and has filled the whole world with His teaching? Let the Greeks tell us, who mock at Him without stint or shame. If He is a man, how is it that one man has proved stronger than all those whom they themselves regard as gods, and by His own power has shown them to be nothing? If they call Him a magician, how is it that by a magician all magic is destroyed, instead of being rendered strong? Had He conquered certain magicians or proved Himself superior to one of them only, they might reasonably think that He excelled the rest only by His greater skill. But the fact is that His cross has vanquished all magic entirely and has conquered the very name of it. Obviously, therefore, the Saviour is no magician, for the very demons whom the magicians invoke flee from Him as from their Master. Who is He, then? Let the Greeks tell us, whose only serious pursuit is mockery! Perhaps they will say that He, too, is a demon, and that is why He prevailed. But even so the laugh is still on our side. for we can confute them by the same proofs as before. How could He be a demon, Who drives demons out? If it were only certain ones that He drove out, then they might reasonably think that He prevailed against them through the power of their Chief, as the Jews, wishing to insult Him, actually said. But since the fact is, here again, that at the mere naming of His Name all madness of the demons is rooted out and put to flight, obviously the

Greeks are wrong here, too, and our Lord and Saviour Christ is not, as they maintain, some demonic power.

If, then, the Saviour is neither a mere man nor a magician, nor one of the demons, but has by His Godhead confounded and overshadowed the opinions of the poets and the delusion of the demons and the wisdom of the Greeks, it must be manifest and will be owned by all that He is in truth Son of God, Existent Word and Wisdom and Power of the Father. This is the reason why His works are no mere human works, but, both intrinsically and by comparison with those of men, are recognized as being superhuman and truly the works of God.

1.8.49 What man that ever was, for instance, formed a body for himself from a virgin only? Or what man ever healed so many diseases as the common Lord of all? Who restored that which was lacking in man's nature or made one blind from birth to see? Aesculapius was deified by the Greeks because he practiced the art of healing and discovered herbs as remedies for bodily diseases, not, of course, forming them himself out of the earth, but finding them out by the study of nature. But what is that in comparison with what the Saviour did when, instead of just healing a wound, He both fashioned essential being and restored to health the thing that He had formed? Hercules, too, is worshipped as a god by the Greeks because he fought against other men and destroyed wild animals by craft. But what is that to what the Word did, in driving away from men diseases and demons and even death itself? Dionysus is worshipped among them, because he taught men drunkenness; yet they ridicule the true Saviour and Lord of all, Who taught men temperance.

That, however, is enough on this point. What will they say to the other marvels of His Godhead? At what man's death was the sun darkened and the earth shaken? Why, even to this day men are dying, and they did so also before that time. When did any such marvels happen in their case? Now shall we pass over the deeds done in His earthly body and mention those after His resurrection? Has any man's teaching, in any place or at any time, ever prevailed everywhere as one and the same, from one end of the earth to the other, so that his worship has fairly flown through every land? Again, if, as they say, Christ is man only and not God the Word, why do not the gods of the Greeks prevent His entering their domains? Or why, on the other hand, does the Word Himself dwelling in our midst make an end of their worship by His teaching and put their fraud to shame?

1.8.50 Many before Him have been kings and tyrants of the earth, history tells also of many among the Chaldeans and Egyptians and Indians who were wise men and magicians. But which of those, I do not say after his death, but while yet in this life, was ever able so far to prevail as to fill the whole world with his teaching and retrieve so great a multitude from the craven fear of idols, as our Saviour has won over from idols to Himself? The Greek philosophers have compiled many works with persuasiveness and much skill in words; but what fruit have they to show for this such as has the cross of Christ? Their wise thoughts were persuasive enough until they died; yet even in their life-time their seeming influence was counterbalanced by their rivalry with one another, for they were a jealous company and declaimed against each other. But the Word of God, by strangest paradox, teaching in meaner language, has put the choicest sophists in the shade, and by confounding their teachings and drawing all men to Himself He has filled His own assemblies. Moreover, and this is the marvelous thing by going down as Man to death He has confounded all the sounding utterances of the wise men about the idols. For whose death ever drove out demons, or whose death did ever demons fear, save that of Christ? For where the Saviour is named, there every demon is driven out. Again, who has ever so rid men of their natural passions that fornicators become chaste and murderers no longer wield the sword and those who formerly were craven cowards boldly play the man? In a word, what persuaded the barbarians and heathen folk in every place to drop their madness and give heed to peace, save the faith of Christ and the sign of the cross? What other things have given men such certain faith in immortality as have the cross of Christ and the resurrection of His body? The Greeks told all sorts of false tales, but they could never pretend that their idols rose again from death: indeed it never entered their heads that a body could exist again after death at all. And one would be particularly ready to listen to them on this point, because by these opinions they have exposed the weakness of their own idolatry, at the same time yielding to Christ the possibility of bodily resurrection, so that by that means He might be recognized by all as Son of God.

1.8.51 Again, who among men, either after his death or while yet living, taught about virginity and did not account this virtue impossible for human beings? But Christ our Saviour and King of all has so prevailed with His teaching on this subject that even children not yet of lawful age promise that virginity which transcends the law. And who among men has ever been able to penetrate even to Scythians and Ethiopians, or Parthians or Armenians or those who are said to live beyond Hyrcania, or even the Egyptians and Chaldeans, people who give heed to magic and are more than naturally enslaved by the fear of demons and savage in their habits, and to preach at all about virtue and self-control and against the worshipping of idols, as has the Lord of all, the Power of God, our Lord Jesus Christ? Yet He not only preached through His own disciples, but also wrought so persuasively on men's understanding that, laying aside their savage habits and forsaking the worship of their ancestral gods, they learnt to know Him and through Him to worship the Father. While they were yet idolaters, the Greeks and Barbarians were always at war with each other, and were even cruel to their own kith and kin. Nobody could travel by land or sea at all unless he was armed with swords, because of their irreconcilable quarrels with each other. Indeed, the whole course of their life was carried on with the weapons, and the sword with them replaced the staff and was the mainstay of all aid. All this time, as I said before, they were serving idols and offering sacrifices to demons, and for all the superstitious awe that accompanied this idol worship, nothing could wean them from that warlike spirit. But, strange to relate, since they came over to the school of Christ, as men moved with real compunction they have laid aside their murderous cruelty and are war-minded no more. On the contrary, all is peace among them and nothing remains save desire for friendship.

1.8.52 Who, then, is He Who has done these things and has united in peace those who hated each other, save the beloved Son of the Father, the common Saviour of all, Jesus Christ, Who by His own love underwent all things for our salvation? Even from the beginning, moreover, this peace that He was to administer was foretold, for Scripture says, "They shall beat their swords into plough-shares and their spears into sickles, and nation shall not take sword against nation, neither shall they learn any more to wage war."[65] Nor is this by any means incredible.

The barbarians of the present day are naturally savage in their habits, and as long as they sacrifice to their idols they rage furiously against each other and cannot bear to be a single hour without weapons. But when they hear the teaching of Christ, forthwith they turn from

---

65   Isaiah 2:4

fighting to farming, and instead of arming themselves with swords extend their hands in prayer. In a word, instead of fighting each other, they take up arms against the devil and the demons, and overcome them by their self-command and integrity of soul. These facts are proof of the Godhead of the Saviour, for He has taught men what they could never learn among the idols. It is also no small exposure of the weakness and nothingness of demons and idols, for it was because they knew their own weakness that the demons were always setting men to fight each other, fearing lest, if they ceased from mutual strife, they would turn to attack the demons themselves. For in truth the disciples of Christ, instead of fighting each other, stand arrayed against demons by their habits and virtuous actions, and chase them away and mock at their captain the devil. Even in youth they are chaste, they endure in times of testing and persevere in toils. When they are insulted, they are patient, when robbed they make light of it, and, marvelous to relate, they make light even of death itself, and become martyrs of Christ.

1.8.53 And here is another proof of the Godhead of the Saviour, which is indeed utterly amazing. What mere man or magician or tyrant or king was ever able by himself to do so much? Did anyone ever fight against the whole system of idol-worship and the whole host of demons and all magic and all the wisdom of the Greeks, at a time when all of these were strong and flourishing and taking everybody in, as did our Lord, the very Word of God? Yet He is even now invisibly exposing every man's error, and single-handed is carrying off all men from them all, so that those who used to worship idols now tread them under foot, reputed magicians burn their books and the wise prefer to all studies the interpretation of the gospels. They are deserting those whom formerly they worshipped, they worship and confess as Christ and God Him Whom they used to ridicule as crucified. Their so-called gods are routed by the sign of the cross, and the crucified Saviour is proclaimed in all the world as God and Son of God. Moreover, the gods worshipped among the Greeks are now falling into disrepute among them on account of the disgraceful things they did, for those who receive the teaching of Christ are more chaste in life than they. If these, and the like of them, are human works, let anyone who will show us similar ones done by men in former time, and so convince us. But if they are shown to be, and are the works not of men but of God, why are the unbelievers so irreligious as not to recognize the Master Who did them? They are afflicted as a man would be who failed to recognize God the Artificer through the works of creation. For surely if they had recognized His Godhead through His power over the universe, they would recognize also that the bodily works of Christ are not human, but are those of the Saviour of all, the Word of God. And had they recognized this, as Paul says, "They would not have crucified the Lord of glory."[66]

---

66 1 Corinthians 2:8

1.8.54 As, then, he who desires to see God Who by nature is invisible and not to be beheld, may yet perceive and know Him through His works, so too let him who does not see Christ with his understanding at least consider Him in His bodily works and test whether they be of man or God. If they be of man, then let him scoff; but if they be of God, let him not mock at things which are no fit subject for scorn, but rather let him recognize the fact and marvel that things divine have been revealed to us by such humble means, that through death deathlessness has been made known to us, and through the Incarnation of the Word the Mind whence all things proceed has been declared, and its Agent and Ordainer, the Word of God Himself. He, indeed, assumed humanity that we might become God. He manifested Himself by means of a body in order that we might perceive the Mind of the unseen Father. He endured shame from men that we might inherit immortality. He Himself was unhurt by this, for He is impassable and incorruptible; but by His own impassability He kept and healed the suffering men on whose account He thus endured. In short, such and so many are the Saviour's achievements that follow from His Incarnation, that to try to number them is like gazing at the open sea and trying to count the waves. One cannot see all the waves with one's eyes, for when one tries to do so those that are following on baffle one's senses. Even so, when one wants to take in all the achievements of Christ in the body, one cannot do so, even by reckoning them up, for the things that transcend one's thought are always more than those one thinks that one has grasped.

As we cannot speak adequately about even a part of His work, therefore, it will be better for us not to speak about it as a whole. So we will mention but one thing more, and then leave the whole for you to marvel at. For, indeed, everything about it is marvelous, and wherever a man turns his gaze he sees the Godhead of the Word and is smitten with awe.

1.8.55 The substance of what we have said so far may be summarized as follows. Since the Saviour came to dwell among us, not only does idolatry no longer increase, but it is getting less and gradually ceasing to be. Similarly, not only does the wisdom of the Greeks no longer make any progress, but that which used to be is disappearing. And demons, so far from continuing to impose on people by their deceits and oracle-givings and sorceries, are routed by the sign of the cross if they so much as try. On the other hand, while idolatry and everything else that opposes the faith of Christ is daily dwindling and weakening and falling, see, the Saviour's teaching is increasing everywhere! Worship, then, the Saviour "Who is above all" and mighty, even God the Word, and condemn those who are being defeated and made to disappear by Him. When the sun has come, darkness prevails no longer; any of it that may be left anywhere is driven away. So also, now that the Divine epiphany of the Word of God has taken place, the darkness of idols prevails no more, and all parts of the world in every direction are enlightened by His teaching. Similarly, if a king be reigning somewhere, but stays in his own house and does not let himself be seen, it often happens that some insubordinate fellows, taking advantage of his retirement, will have themselves proclaimed in his stead; and each of them, being invested with the semblance of kingship, misleads the simple who, because they cannot enter the palace and see the real king, are led astray by just hearing a king named. When the real king emerges, however, and appears to view, things stand differently. The insubordinate impostors are shown up by his presence, and men, seeing the real king, forsake those who previously misled them. In the same way the demons used formerly to impose on men, investing themselves with the honour due to God. But since the Word of God has been manifested in a body, and has made known to us His own Father, the fraud of the demons is stopped and made to disappear; and men, turning their eyes to the true God, Word of the Father, forsake the idols and come to know the true God.

Now this is proof that Christ is God, the Word and Power of God. For whereas human things cease and the fact of Christ remains, it is clear to all that the things which cease are temporary, but that He Who remains is God and very Son of God, the sole-begotten Word.

1.9 Conclusion

1.9.56 Here, then, Macarius, is our offering to you who love Christ, a brief statement of the faith of Christ and of the manifestation of His Godhead to us. This will give you a beginning, and you must go on to prove its truth by the study of the Scriptures. They were written and inspired by God; and we, who have learned from inspired teachers who read the Scriptures and became martyrs for the Godhead of Christ, make further contribution to your eagerness to learn. From the Scriptures you will learn also of His second manifestation to us, glorious and divine indeed, when He shall come not in lowliness but in His proper glory, no longer in humiliation but in majesty, no longer to suffer but to bestow on us all the fruit of His cross – the resurrection and incorruptibility. No longer will He then be judged, but rather will Himself be Judge, judging each and all according to their deeds done in the body, whether good or ill. Then for the good is laid up the heavenly kingdom, but for those that practice evil outer darkness and the eternal fire. So also the Lord Himself says, "I say unto you, hereafter ye shall see the Son of Man seated on the right hand of power, coming on the clouds of heaven in the glory of the Father."[67] For that Day we have one of His own sayings to prepare us, "Get ready and watch, for ye know not the hour in which He cometh"[68] And blessed Paul says, "We must all stand before the judgment seat of Christ, that each one may receive according as he practiced in the body, whether good or ill."[69]

---

67 Matthew 26:64
68 Matthew 24:42
69 2 Corinthians 5:10

1.9.57 But for the searching and right understanding of the Scriptures there is need of a good life and a pure soul, and for Christian virtue to guide the mind to grasp, so far as human nature can, the truth concerning God the Word. One cannot possibly understand the teaching of the saints unless one has a pure mind and is trying to imitate their life. Anyone who wants to look at sunlight naturally wipes his eye clear first, in order to make, at any rate, some approximation to the purity of that on which he looks; and a person wishing to see a city or country goes to the place in order to do so. Similarly, anyone who wishes to understand the mind of the sacred writers must first cleanse his own life, and approach the saints by copying their deeds. Thus united to them in the fellowship of life, he will both understand the things revealed to them by God and, thenceforth escaping the peril that threatens sinners in the judgment, will receive that which is laid up for the saints in the kingdom of heaven. Of that reward it is written: "Eye hath not seen nor ear heard, neither hath entered into the heart of man the things that God has prepared"[70] for them that live a godly life and love the God and Father in Christ Jesus our Lord, through Whom and with Whom be to the Father Himself, with the Son Himself, in the Holy Spirit, honour and might and glory to ages of ages. Amen.

---

70 1 Corinthians 2:9

About the Contributor(s)

Steven R. Martins is a Christian thinker and writer, founding director of the Cantaro Institute and church planter in St. Catharines. A second-generation Canadian, Steven is of Ibero-American parentage and has worked in the fields of missional apologetics and church leadership for eight years. He has spoken at numerous conferences, churches, and University student events, from York University, Toronto, to the University of West Indies in Port of Spain, Trinidad, and the national Universities of Costa Rica (UNCR and UNC) and the Evangelical University of El Salvador. He has also contributed articles to Coalición por el Evangelio (TGC in Spanish) and the Siglo XXI journal of Editorial CLIR.

Steven holds a Master's degree *summa cum laude* in Theological Studies with a focus on Christian apologetics from Veritas International University (Santa Ana, CA., USA) and a Bachelor of Human Resource Management from York University (Toronto, ON., Canada). Steven presently serves on the executive board for Answers in Genesis Canada, and has served with the Ezra Institute for Contemporary Christianity (EICC) as a staff apologist, writer and director of ministry development and advancement (DMDA) for four years. He has also served pastorally at Harbour Fellowship Church in St. Catharines for two years. Steven is married to Cindy and they live in Jordan Station, Ontario, with their son Matthias.